More social studies titles in the
Inquire and Investigate series

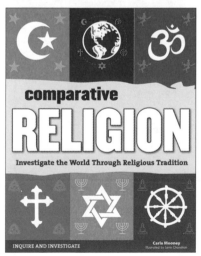

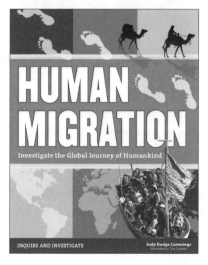

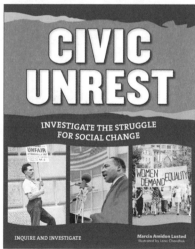

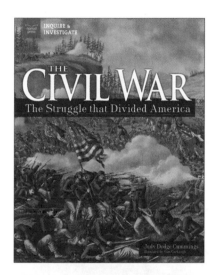

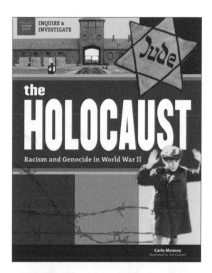

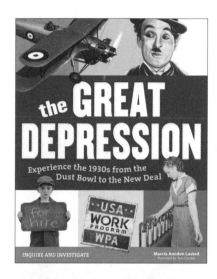

Interested in primary sources?

(PS)

Look for this icon.

You can use a smartphone or tablet app to scan the QR codes and explore more! Cover up neighboring QR codes to make sure you're scanning the right one. You can find a list of URLs on the Resources page.

If the QR code doesn't work, try searching the Internet with the Keyword Prompts to find other helpful sources.

 Terrorism

What are source notes?

In this book, you'll find small numbers at the end of some paragraphs. These numbers indicate that you can find source notes for that section in the back of the book. Source notes tell readers where the writer got their information. This might be a news article, a book, or another kind of media. Source notes are a way to know that what you are reading is true information that other people have verified. They can also lead you to more places where you explore a topic that you're curious about!

Contents ▶

TIMELINE

66 to 73 CE..................... A Jewish sect called the Zealots fight against the Roman Empire's occupation of the land that is now known as Israel.

1000s and 1100s........... In Iran and Syria, a group known as the Assassins sends members on suicide missions to murder enemy leaders in its struggle to overthrow Sunni leaders in Islam.

1789............................... The French Revolution overthrows the monarchy and establishes a new government. The new French state orders enemies of the state killed, an early example of state-sanctioned terror.

1964............................... The Palestine Liberation Organization begins fighting to establish a Palestinian state.

1968............................... The Provisional Irish Republican Army is formed with a goal to end British rule in Northern Ireland and to reunify Ireland as a Catholic country.

1978–1995..................... American Unabomber Ted Kaczynski anonymously delivers 16 mail bombs that kill three people and injure 23 others.

1983............................... Suicide bombers attack the U.S. embassy in Beirut, Lebanon, killing 63 people. The attack marks the beginning of anti-U.S. attacks by Islamist groups.

1987............................... Harakat al-Muqawama al-Islamiya, better known as Hamas, is founded in the West Bank and Gaza in the Middle East in the struggle for an Islamic fundamentalist Palestinian state.

1988............................... A terrorist bomb explodes on Pan Am Flight 103 flying from Frankfurt, Germany, to Detroit, Michigan, killing all on board. Terrorists from Libya are blamed for the bombing, known as the Lockerbie bombing.

1995............................... Members of the Aum Shinrikyo cult movement release sarin, a powerful nerve gas, on several subway lines in Tokyo, Japan, killing 12 people and injuring hundreds more.

1995............................... Timothy McVeigh and Terry Nichols detonate a truck bomb in front of the Alfred P. Murrah Federal Building in Oklahoma City, Oklahoma, killing 168 people and injuring hundreds more. To date, it is the deadliest domestic terrorism attack in U.S. history.

1996............................... The U.S. Congress passes the Antiterrorism and Effective Death Penalty Act, the country's first comprehensive counterterrorism legislation.

1998............................... Osama bin Laden forms the Al-Qaeda terrorist group.

TIMELINE

2001 . . . . Nineteen terrorists from Al-Qaeda hijack four commercial airplanes on September 11, deliberately crashing two of the planes into the World Trade Center towers in New York City and a third plane into the Pentagon in Arlington, Virginia. The fourth plane crashes in Pennsylvania.

2001 . . . . The United Nations passes Security Council Resolution 1373, an international response to the 9/11 terrorist attacks. It also creates the UN Counterterrorism Committee.

2002 . . . . The U.S. Department of Homeland Security is created and the USA Patriot Act is signed into law. Both are designed to improve the ability of the United States to fight terrorism.

2005 . . . . Islamic extremists detonate three bombs on London, England, subway trains and a fourth on a double-decker bus, killing 52 people and injuring more than 700 others.

2011 . . . . American Special Forces kill Osama bin Laden.

2013 . . . . Dzhokhar and Tamerlan Tsarnaev detonate two homemade bombs at the finish line of the Boston Marathon in Massachusetts, killing three people and injuring several hundred.

2015 . . . . Three suicide bombers strike near the Stade de France outside Paris, France, followed by suicide bombings and mass shootings at cafés, restaurants, and a music venue in central Paris, killing 130 people and injuring more than 350 others. The attacks are the deadliest in France since World War II.

2015 . . . . A white supremacist named Dylann Roof enters an African-American church in Charleston, South Carolina, and opens fire on parishioners who had gathered for Bible study. Roof kills nine people, all African Americans.

2016 . . . . Omar Mateen enters a gay nightclub in Orlando, Florida, shooting and killing 49 people and injuring 53 others.

2016 . . . . A cargo truck drives into crowds celebrating Bastille Day in Nice, France, killing 86 people and injuring 434 more. The attack is linked to the Islamic State/ISIS.

2017 . . . . A suicide bombing occurs at Manchester Arena in Manchester, England, following a concert by singer Ariana Grande, killing 22 people and injuring more than 100 others. The attacker, Salman Ramadan Abedi, is a 22-year-old British citizen suspected of being connected to Islamic State/ISIS.

A Day the World Will Not Forget

How does terrorism
affect people
around the world?

Terrorists use violence to advance their goals by causing victims to feel fear, hopelessness, and loss, which can make people less likely to take a stand against policies they perceive as wrong.

Terrorism is a global phenomenon that affects many people worldwide and has a long history, dating back to ancient societies. For generations, terrorist attacks have been carried out against people of all nationalities and ethnic and religious backgrounds.

Recent terrorist attacks in Belgium, California, and France demonstrate that the threat of terrorism continues. Who are the terrorists? What are their motives? And how can we stop the violence? These are questions that people around the world are trying to answer as we attempt to understand this deadly tool of intimidation.

For many people in the United States, the problem of terrorism became a personal one when the country suffered the deadliest terror attack in its history.

SEPTEMBER 11

Tuesday, September 11, 2001, began as an ordinary day. Workers at the World Trade Center in New York City arrived at their offices, sipped their morning coffee, and logged onto their computers. As they followed their normal routines, they did not know that their lives, and the lives of millions of people around the world, were about to change.

At 8:46 in the morning, a hijacked commercial airplane flew directly into the North Tower of the World Trade Center. The impact triggered a massive explosion. At first, people were confused and thought it was a small plane accident. At 9:03, as national news channels broadcast breaking news about the first crash, a second commercial airplane crashed into the South Tower. In less than two hours, both towers collapsed, killing nearly 2,800 people.

Beyond New York City, other attacks occurred that same morning. At 9:37, a third hijacked airplane struck the Pentagon in Arlington, Virginia.

Recognizing that the country was under attack, the Federal Aviation Administration immediately grounded all commercial and private planes in the United States. Thousands of flights in the air were ordered to land at the nearest airport. Cities around the country evacuated major buildings and closed bridges, roads, and other public spaces. Meanwhile, a fourth hijacked plane crashed near Shanksville, Pennsylvania, killing all on board.

A SURVIVOR'S STORY

John Mahony was working on the 19th floor of the North Tower when the first plane hit. Upon impact, the building jerked hard, throwing Mahony and his coworkers off balance. Mahony, who had lived in California, thought the jerking felt like an earthquake.

PRIMARY SOURCES

Primary sources come from people who were eyewitnesses to events. They might write about the event, take pictures, post short messages to social media or blogs, or record the event for radio or video. The photographs in this book are primary sources, taken at the time of the event. Paintings of events are usually not primary sources, since they were often painted long after the event took place. What other primary sources can you find? Why are primary sources important? Do you learn differently from primary sources than from secondary sources, which come from people who did not directly experience the event?

A retired Army colonel, Mahony's military training kicked in and he began directing coworkers to the nearest stairway. Along with hundreds of other people, Mahony slowly made his way down the stairs through a haze of smoke and dust. At one point, the fire sprinklers turned on and people had to grab the handrails to keep from being swept off their feet by the torrent of water flowing down the stairs. On the way down, Mahony passed several firefighters climbing up the stairs, going higher into the tower.

When Mahony reached the ground floor, he found chaos. Rubble was strewn all over the lobby and elevators. Injured and panicked people called for help. One injured woman cried as a coworker carried her over his back. Another woman was so badly burned that Mahony could not tell her original skin color. A firefighter directed him to a side door, telling him that he could not use the front door because people were jumping from the upper floors.

Outside the building, the street looked like a post-apocalyptic movie.

Cars burned and chunks of metal and glass littered the street. Shoes were strewn everywhere. As Mahony crossed the street, the sound of jet engines roared above. That's when the second plane hit the South Tower. As he watched in horror, the building seemed to absorb the plane. Then the tower's glass wall rippled. Glass and jet fuel exploded and poured down the side of the building.

Mahony ran to escape the falling glass and other refuse. After a few blocks, he turned to look at the towers again. He saw hundreds of people jumping to their deaths from the upper floors of the building. Then, the first tower collapsed and sent out an enormous cloud of ash and detritus that flowed for blocks.

VOCAB LAB

There is a lot of new vocabulary in this book. Turn to the glossary in the back when you come to a word you don't understand. Practice your new vocabulary in the **VOCAB LAB** activities in each chapter.

As the debris cloud reached him, cement particles covered Mahony, entering his nose, eyes, and ears. Trapped on the south side of the towers, at Battery Park, Mahony saw the second tower begin to fall.

A DEVASTATING ATTACK

The September 11 (9/11), 2001, terrorist attacks in New York City, Arlington, Virginia, and Pennsylvania changed the world. The attacks pushed terrorism into the spotlight and triggered a series of global events that included the invasion of Afghanistan and the Iraq War. In addition to the 2,996 people killed on 9/11, more than 6,000 people were wounded.

For many, the visible and invisible scars of that day will be carried for a lifetime. Although John Mahony and others survived, they lost numerous friends and coworkers. Many survivors faced health and psychological issues. Countless people have dealt with post-traumatic stress syndrome after the attacks. Others have struggled with physical health issues. The smoke and debris that Mahony inhaled on 9/11 have left him with health problems that could shorten his life.

WHO IS AL-QAEDA?

Years later, in a message aired on an Arabic television station in October 2004, Al-Qaeda leader Osama bin Laden appeared and publicly claimed responsibility for the September 11 attacks on the United States. He explained that his radical Islamic group decided to destroy the American towers for several reasons. These included protesting American support of the country of Israel and the American presence in Saudi Arabia.

Bin Laden formed Al-Qaeda in 1988, working with other Arabs who fought against the Soviet Union in Afghanistan. The militant group declared its goal to be the establishment of a pan-Islamic caliphate throughout the Muslim world. In addition, Al-Qaeda sought to unite Muslims to fight against the West and, in particular, against the United States. The group wanted to remove Western influences from Muslim countries and to defeat Israel. In a February 1998 statement, Al-Qaeda claimed that it was the duty of all Muslims to kill Americans and their allies around the world—including civilians.

Al-Qaeda does not speak for the majority of Muslims, most of whom are peaceful and productive citizens of many different countries.

In addition to the 9/11 attacks, Al-Qaeda and its affiliates have carried out terrorist attacks around the world. The group has claimed responsibility for the October 2000 attack on the USS *Cole* in Yemen, which killed 17 American sailors and injured 39. The 1998 bombings at the U.S. embassies in Kenya and Tanzania, which killed 224 and injured more than 5,000 people, were also coordinated by Al-Qaeda.

In 2011, American special forces killed Osama bin Laden. The militant group moved quickly to name Ayman al-Zawahiri as their new leader. Although Al-Qaeda's influence has diminished in recent years, the U.S. National Counterterrorism Center warns that the group continues to plot additional attacks against the United States at home and overseas.

A GLOBAL PROBLEM

Terrorism: Violence, Intimidation, and Solutions for Peace examines both the history of terrorism and its current forms. Topics include the causes of terrorism, the effects of terrorism on countries and communities, the psychology of recruiting, who is attracted to it, and how they become engaged. We'll explore how terrorism is defined and the motives and methods behind it.

The text and activities in *Terrorism* will encourage you to think critically about current and future efforts to prevent terrorist attacks. By understanding the history and motivations that drive terrorism, you will gain a better understanding of how and why terrorists use violence to intimidate people around the world.

KEY QUESTIONS

- In what ways does terrorism result in long-term problems for individuals, families, and communities?

- What were some of the reasons Al-Qaeda attacked the United States?

- Does your school or community mark the anniversary of 9/11 in any way? How do these events make you feel?

- Why does Al-Qaeda claim to speak for all Muslims? How does that lie help its cause?

WHERE WERE YOU WHEN?

Many people in middle school and high school don't have memories of the 9/11 attacks because the event happened before they were born or when they were too young to form memories of it. You can learn a lot about the personal impact of terrorism by asking people where they were and what they remember about the attacks.

- **Arrange to talk to someone about what they remember about September 11.** This could be a parent, a teacher, or another adult. Before meeting with them, create a list of questions to ask. You might include some of the following.

  - Where were you when you heard about the 9/11 attacks?

  - How did you hear about them?

  - What do you remember the most about that day?

  - What are some of the emotions that you felt on 9/11?

  - How did your life change because of that day?

- **You can use a recording device or take notes while you talk with your interview subject.** Make sure they are comfortable with being recorded.

  - What do you learn from your conversation?

  - Does the interview make you think differently about the events?

To investigate more, create a presentation based on your interview. You might use PowerPoint or create a graphic novel or a painting. How does your work reflect the emotions that your subject felt about the terrorist attack? How do they reflect your own emotions? How do we acknowledge the emotions that arise when we think about terrorism while still focusing on the problem critically and creatively?

Chapter 1 ▶

Defining Terrorism

Why is it difficult to define terrorism?

Terrorism has different meanings for different people, and a certain act might be considered terrorism by some groups but not by others. This makes it difficult for the world to agree on one definition.

What is terrorism? Terrorism has existed for centuries, but it's not easy to define. Terrorism is different from war. In war, countries openly declare war on each other and fight in battles. Instead, terrorism is the use of violence against civilians in order to achieve political or social goals. But this definition might not mean the same thing in every country.

Who are considered civilians? What are the goals that the terrorists are working toward? If one person murders another person for money, is that an act of terrorism?

In the United States, the Federal Bureau of Investigation (FBI) defines terrorism as "the unlawful use of force or violence against persons or property to intimidate or coerce a government, the civilian population, or any segment thereof, in furtherance of political or social objectives."

What does this mean?

Using the FBI's definition, terrorism is always violent, which makes it different from the peaceful work of political parties or other organizations. Unlike a military attack, which targets an opposing military force or infrastructure, such as a bridge or ship, a terrorist attack targets ordinary civilians, including the elderly, women, and children. Often, these attacks are stealthy and surprising for unsuspecting targets.

It's important to remember that terrorism is used to achieve a specific goal, often a political or social goal. For example, a terrorist group might engage in violent actions to achieve the political goal of overthrowing an enemy government. Some terrorist actions are attempts to call attention to a cause. Some attacks are designed to weaken a society or government. Other terrorist actions may be intended to harm an economy or provoke military action.

When terrorists attack American citizens, they might believe their actions will force the U.S. government to take away the freedoms and rights of U.S. citizens. This loss of freedoms could damage American society. For some terrorists, the goal is simply to spread fear among a people, which can have harmful implications for many years to come.

ROOTED IN EXTREMISM

To define terrorism, it is helpful to take a look at a related idea: extremism. A person who is an extremist holds extreme political or religious views and expresses them in radical ways. An extremist often presents their views in an uncompromising, bullying way. Extremists are frequently intolerant toward people who oppose their ideas or have different opinions.

MASSACRE AT THE 1972 OLYMPICS

In 1972, the Black September Organization, a Palestinian terrorist group, used the worldwide platform of the Olympic Games to bring attention to the struggle of Palestinian refugees. At the 1972 Games in Munich, West Germany, members of the terrorist group entered the athletes' village in the middle of the night. They killed two and captured nine members of the Israeli Olympic team. In exchange for the release of the Israeli hostages, the terrorists demanded the release of more than 200 Palestinians and other non-Arabs jailed in Israel. When a gun battle erupted between the kidnappers and West German police, the terrorists murdered the remaining nine hostages.

While an extremist's views might be hateful, they are not terrorists if their actions are not violent. Some extremists express their views non-violently by sponsoring debates or publishing newspapers. Others hold rallies or events.

For example, in March 1998, the American Knights of the Ku Klux Klan (AK-KKK) held a rally near Pittsburgh, Pennsylvania. The AK-KKK was an activist faction of the KKK during the 1990s. They believed in white racial supremacy. To express these beliefs, they held rallies at government sites. Although their speeches were racist, hateful, and inflammatory, they did not promote or encourage violence.

No matter how offensive a person's thoughts or words are, thoughts and words are not acts of terrorism. Some extremists might vandalize targets or disrupt the routines of their opponents. While these activities can be disruptive and sometimes illegal, they are not usually considered terrorist acts.

Members of the Ku Klux Klan gather to support a Republican presidential candidate while an African American pushes back their signs

credit: Library of Congress

VIOLENT EXTREMISTS

When extremist behavior becomes violent, it crosses the line into terrorism. Terrorists often use their extreme beliefs to justify violent acts. Terrorism experts have identified several common characteristics of extremists who turn to violence. These people are often extremely intolerant of different opinions, see the world in moral absolutes, reach broad conclusions about others, use coded language, and often hold different worldviews from those who do not share their beliefs.

Many extremists who turn violent are intolerant of those who hold differing beliefs and views. They view their cause as the only one that is right and just. Violent extremists also typically see the world in moral absolutes. This means that in their view, the lines between good and evil are crystal clear—they stand in the right, while their opponents are wrong.

Anyone who disagrees with them is considered an opponent.

This viewpoint gives them moral superiority over those who do not share their beliefs and causes. For example, religious terrorists believe that their faith is the one true faith and is superior to all others. Any act taken to defend the faith, even if it is violent, is justified because it is on the side of right.

Many violent extremists also make broad conclusions and generalizations about others, often believing that an entire group of people has negative traits. No debate or exceptions to these generalizations are permitted. They might generalize that all people in the opponent group are greedy and immoral. Of course, it's rare that every member of any group will share those characteristics.

GUERRILLA WARFARE

In most definitions, terrorism is not the same as guerrilla warfare. Guerrilla fighters are armed people who operate as a military unit. Unlike terrorists who target civilians, guerrilla fighters usually attack enemy military forces. Often outnumbered by enemy forces, they typically attack in a hit-and-run style, moving quickly in small, mobile units. During the Holocaust, small guerilla units of Jewish fighters called partisans hid and lived in the dense forests of Eastern Europe. The partisans planned quick attacks and sabotage on Nazi targets.

In some cases, violent extremists use new or coded language. For example, some Neo-Nazi groups call non-European races "mud people." Using this language sets them apart from others who do not share their beliefs.

> For extremists, their beliefs and terrorist actions are completely logical.

Extremists who turn to violence often see the world very differently. In their eyes, they take the role of protectors of a truth, religion, or government. They frequently believe that secret forces are working against them. For example, some racial extremists believe that international Judaism controls the world's banking system and runs governments in countries such as France and the United States. This worldview sets the extremist apart from other people and gives them a clear sense of mission, purpose, and righteousness.

FORMS OF TERRORISM

Throughout history, terrorism has taken several forms. In fact, one of the reasons terrorism can be so difficult to define is because it can appear in a variety of ways.

The terrorist attacks on September 11 were rooted in religion. The men who organized and carried out the attacks held extreme religious views. They considered anyone who held different views as an enemy. They believed that the West, especially the United States, was an enemy to their own religion, Islam. They believed that their extreme actions, even against civilians, were justified to protect Islam from its enemies and spread its true faith. This form of terrorism, called religious terrorism, has occurred throughout history.

Religious terrorists of different faiths carry out violent acts because they believe these actions will protect and defend their faith.

Sometimes, governments engage in or sponsor terrorist acts, usually directed against enemies of the state, both outside the country and within its borders. States even sponsor terrorist groups in other countries to support their own interests. For example, the government of Iran has supported the militant group Hezbollah, which operates in Lebanon against Israel. Other times, dissident groups violently attack governments, religious groups, ethnic or national groups, and others.

Sometimes, profit or a combination of profit and politics pushes criminal terrorists to act. Organized crime groups, such as the Italian Mafia, have engaged in terroristic acts to protect their profits from other criminal activity.

TERRORIST OR FREEDOM FIGHTER?

Sometimes, the line between a terrorist and freedom fighter is blurred. What makes one person a terrorist, while another is a freedom fighter struggling against oppression? Often, the answer depends on your point of view.

According to Richard Betts, the director of the Institute of War and Peace Studies at Columbia University, the main issue is that many people believe there are situations where extreme actions are justified. For example, the United States bombed civilian targets in World War II, but few people call those actions terrorism.

Instead, the U.S. actions were part of a military operation. After the United States was attacked by Japan at Pearl Harbor, it was drawn into a war with aggressor nations.

Do terrorists know they're terrorists? Many people and organizations whose activities fit the definition of terrorism will deny that they are terrorists. Instead, they often describe themselves as "freedom fighters" or "revolutionaries."

IMPACT FACT

In 2014, approximately 13,472 people were murdered in the United States. During that same year, only 24 private citizens died worldwide from terrorist attacks.

Hezbollah is an Islamic militant group and political party based in Lebanon. Many people in the West consider Hezbollah to be a terrorist organization because of its rocket attacks against Israeli civilians and towns and attacks against Westerners, including Americans. However, Sheikh Mohammed Hussein Fadlallah, a former religious leader with Hezbollah, had a different view. He explained that, "The Americans believe in democracy, and they should know that we are not terrorists, but freedom fighters struggling to get back our occupied lands."[1]

Sometimes, repressive governments accuse opposition groups of being terrorists, even when the rest of the world views these groups as freedom fighters resisting injustice. For example, various militant groups in Nicaragua opposed the socialist Sandinista government from 1979 to the early 1990s. Called the Contras, the groups were often viewed by the United States as freedom fighters against the repressive government, even though some used violent tactics against civilians. By labeling such groups as terrorists, governments can justify any violent acts against the groups.

Atomic cloud over Nagasaki from Koyagi-jima. This atomic bomb was not considered to be a terrorist attack because the United States was at war with Japan.

credit: Hiromichi Matsuda

HISTORY OF TERRORISM

Terrorism has a long history, with the first known, recorded terrorist acts occurring more than 2,000 years ago. At the time, the Zealots of Judea fought against the Roman Empire's occupation of the land known today as Israel.

During the eleventh and twelfth centuries, a group called the Assassins was one of the first to use systematic murder as a political weapon. Operating in Iran and Syria, the Assassins were a faction of Shi'a Islam that fought to overthrow Sunni leaders and replace them with their own. They spread fear and terror by carrying out a number of dramatic murders of Islamic leaders, often sending a single assassin to kill an enemy leader while sacrificing his own life. This is a method similar to today's suicide bombers.

The French Revolution introduced the word "terrorism" into the European vocabulary. In 1789, the French overthrew the monarchy and established a new government as Parisian mobs killed prominent officials and aristocrats. In the early years of the revolution, the new French leaders used violence to impose their radical views on the French citizens. Maximilien Robespierre, one of the heads of the new French state, ordered the enemies of the revolution killed, during a time called the Reign of Terror. He justified the violence as necessary to transform the country from a monarchy to a democracy.

Robespierre stated, "Subdue by terror the enemies of liberty, and you will be right, as founders of the republic." His views have been followed by modern terrorists, who believe that violence can help them create a better government.

TERRORISM ON THE DECLINE

Although terrorism seems to always be in the news, actual terrorist attacks have decreased in recent years. According to the Global Terrorism Database, terrorist attacks in the United States sharply declined between 1970 and 2011, from approximately 475 to fewer than 20 incidents per year. In Western Europe, where many terrorist attacks have occurred, the period from 2000 to 2016 experienced relatively low terrorist activity, as compared to 1970 to 1995. You can see a world map showing the intensity of terrorism attacks in 2016 at this website. Where were the most attacks? Where were the fewest? What else is going on in these different parts of the world that might reveal more about the attacks?

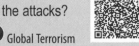

Global Terrorism Database map 2016

In 1968, the modern era of international terrorism arrived when the Popular Front for the Liberation of Palestine hijacked an El Al plane traveling from Tel Aviv, Israel, to Rome, Italy. While hijackings were not new, it was the first time the nationality of the airline carrier and its symbolic meaning was a specific target of a terror group. It was also one of the first times a terror group purposefully used passengers as hostages to negotiate public demands with the Israeli government.

A new type of terrorism came into being in the 1990s.

Osama bin Laden and Al-Qaeda and other religious extremists emerged to resist Western dominance and culture. These terrorist groups had a cause and a network of followers. They were not limited to any one state and their followers were willing to commit suicide to inflict the most damage and destruction on their enemies, as they did on September 11, 2001.

Today, terrorism and terrorists continue to evolve and adapt. Terrorist violence is becoming simpler, and more widespread than the 9/11 attacks. Often, these attacks are carried out by individuals or small groups that may or may not have training. Yet their deadly violence continues to have a significant impact on citizens and countries worldwide.

No single, global definition has been adopted for terrorism. Whether or not you view a violent act as terrorism depends on your perspective. Those people committing violent acts often believe that their actions are justified because they are fighting for the freedom of an oppressed group. For these people, the ends justify the means. For others, violence against innocent civilians is always an act of terror.

KEY QUESTIONS

- "The ends justify the means" is something people might say to justify violence. Do you believe this statement to be true? Why or why not?

- What do you think is the difference between freedom fighters and terrorists? Is it always easy to tell the difference?

HOW DO YOU DEFINE TERRORISM?

Although terrorism seems to be in the news every day, it is not easy to define. Terrorism is different from war, in which countries that have openly declared war on each other fight in battle. It is also different from criminal activity, in which people commit murder, assault, theft, and other crimes for a variety of motives. Each country defines terrorism in its own way. Even within a single country, different agencies or groups might have contrasting definitions of what terrorism is.

- **Use the Internet to explore how different agencies within the United States and countries around the world define terrorism.** Research how each of the following entities define terrorism.

  - European Union

  - United Kingdom

  - United Nations

  - Interpol

  - Human Rights Watch

  - U.S. Department of Defense

  - Federal Bureau of Investigation

  - U.S. Department of State

  - U.S. National Counterterrorism Center

  - USA Patriot Act

- **Compare and contrast each group's definitions.** How are the various definitions similar? How are they different? Why do you think there are differences between the definitions from the different groups? What makes terrorism so difficult to define?

VOCAB LAB

Write down what you think each word means. What root words can you find to help you? What does the context of the word tell you?

civilian, **coerce**, **extremism**, **faction**, **freedom fighter**, **guerrilla warfare**, **Hezbollah**, **infrastructure**, **intolerance**, **justify**, **moral absolutes**, and **repressive**.

Compare your definitions with those of your friends or classmates. Did you all come up with the same meanings? Turn to the text and glossary if you need help.

To investigate more, create your own definition of terrorism. Explain the rationale you used to come up with your definition. Compare your definition with your classmates' definitions.

MAKING A POINT
WITH A CARTOON

A political cartoon expresses an opinion about a political issue or event. This type of cartoon appears in most daily newspapers, typically in the editorial section. Political cartoons can also be found in some magazines and on political websites.

While many political cartoons are funny, the cartoon's main purpose is to persuade the reader. A good political cartoon makes readers think about current events and tries to persuade them to accept the cartoonist's point of view.

- **Political cartoonists use several methods to persuade readers.** When a reader understands how these techniques are used, they can also identify if the cartoonist has a bias regarding an issue. Consider some of these techniques.

  - Symbolism: using objects or symbols to stand for larger ideas.

  - Exaggeration: exaggerating the physical characteristics of a person or object in order to make a point.

  - Labeling: adding labels to objects or people to clearly state what they stand for.

  - Analogy: comparing two unlike objects or situations that share characteristics.

  - Irony: the difference between the way things are and the way they are expected to be.

- **Many political cartoonists have created cartoons that tackle the subject of terrorism.** Find at least three political cartoons in newspapers, magazines, or online that deal with terrorism. You can find some examples here.

 political cartoon terrorism

- **Review each cartoon and consider the following.**

  - What issue related to terrorism does the political cartoon address?

  - What is the cartoonist's opinion on the issue? How do you know?

  - What techniques did the cartoonist use to persuade readers to accept their point of view?

  - Did you find this cartoon persuasive? Why or why not?

  - What other point of view could a reader have on this issue?

One of the most famous political cartoons in history shows England and France carving up the world. J. Gillray, 1805

credit: Library of Congress

To investigate more, create your own political cartoon with a focus on terrorism. What issue will you portray? What is your point of view on that issue? What techniques will you incorporate in the cartoon to persuade readers to agree with your point of view? What other points of view might readers have? After you have finished the cartoon, show it to friends, family, and classmates. Ask them to talk about their reaction to the cartoon.

TERRORIST OR FREEDOM FIGHTER?

Sometimes, it is not clear if a person should be considered a terrorist or a freedom fighter. Some people might see their actions as justified, while others do not. In this activity, you will research a group to explore what makes a terrorist.

- **Choose a historical organization that you want to learn more about.** You can pick one discussed in the chapter or another group, such as Hamas, South Africa's ANC, the Irish Liberation Army, or many others.

- **Research the group online or at the library.**

  - When was the group formed?

  - Is there one leader or many? Who is the leader among the prominent leaders?

  - Who are the group's members? How does the group recruit new members?

  - What are the group's goals? Has the group pursued its goals in other, nonmilitant ways? Have they had success?

  - Who is the group's enemy? What strategies or weapons does the group use against its enemy?

  - What reasons has the group given to justify its actions, choice of targets, and strategy? Does it use religion or another ideology to justify its actions?

  - Is the group attempting to spread fear to force its enemy into acting in a particular way? Has this strategy been successful?

- **Do you believe the group is a terrorist organization?** Explain how you came to your conclusion and what facts support your conclusion.

To investigate more, take another perspective. If you believe the group was not a terrorist organization, look at the information through the eyes of a survivor of one of the group's attacks. If you decided that the group was a terrorist organization, look at the information through the eyes of a supporter. How does changing your perspective affect how you view the information about this group? Does it change your conclusion? Explain why or why not.

Chapter 2 ▶

Who Are the Terrorists?

What might attract a person to the idea that terrorism is the best solution to a problem?

WE CAN SEE THERE ARE TERRORIST GROUPS ON EVERY CONTINENT...

...AND IN A WIDE VARIETY OF COUNTRIES.

SO WHY DO YOU THINK TERRORIST GROUPS EMERGE IN THESE PLACES?

IT CAN HAPPEN ANYWHERE THERE'S A GROUP THAT THINKS IT'S TREATED UNFAIRLY...

...AND THAT SEES VIOLENCE AS ITS ONLY OPTION.

People from all different religions, ethnicities, countries, and political systems become terrorists when they see extreme violence as the only pathway to reaching their goals.

There are millions of people around the world with extreme views on religion, politics, and many other issues. Millions more live under oppressive governments and yearn for freedom or political, social, or religious reforms. Yet only a few of them become terrorists. Why? What causes one person to choose violent action while another does not?

Experts who study terrorism have struggled to identify why people choose terrorist violence. Most believe that there is no single factor that causes a person to choose violent action. Therefore, there is no single portrait of a terrorist. Instead, terrorists are influenced by many different factors.

Terrorists come from a variety of backgrounds, religions, and socio-economic statuses. While many terrorists are men, some are women. Some terrorists are poor and desperate for social and economic change, while others are wealthy and well-educated. Some terrorists come from modern, industrialized countries, while others come from less developed or even impoverished regions.

Terrorism is not exclusive to people of one religion—Christians, Jews, Hindus, and Muslims have all participated in acts of terror.

ETHNO-NATIONALISM

Throughout history, people of different ethnic backgrounds have struggled to live together peacefully. Sometimes, the people of one group believe that they are being treated unfairly and unequally compared to other groups. Other times, a group that was independent in the past now lives under the rule of another ethnic group.

Ethno-nationalism occurs when the people of one ethnic group feel an intense loyalty and devotion to their ethnic group or nation. They place a priority on promoting their group's culture and interests above those of other nations and groups. Why might this be a problem? While some ethno-nationalist groups promote their culture and heritage peacefully, others turn to violence to achieve their goals.

Sometimes, the people of an oppressed ethnic group want to break away from a ruling government and create a state of their own. They might attempt to gain independence through resistance. In some cases, they carry out acts of terror. A disadvantaged group might believe that terrorism is the best way to assert their rights and achieve their goals. They often direct their attacks against targets that symbolize the central government or the majority community.

Many minority groups want to achieve some sort of independence and self-government. Ethno-nationalism is expected to continue to drive terrorism around the world.

An ideology is a system of beliefs, values, and feelings that affect a person's outlook on the world. An ideology is the filter through which a person sees the people and world around them.

IMPACT FACT

What are some of the benefits of a close loyalty to one's heritage?

THE BASQUE CONFLICT

One example of terrorism as a result of ethno-nationalism can be found in the history of the Basques. This ethnic group lives in northern Spain and southern France, at the western end of the Pyrenees mountain range. They speak the Basque language and have their own traditions and culture. For generations, the Basque people ruled themselves and defended themselves against invasions by outsiders. In the Middle Ages, much of their land was taken by other groups, including the Spaniards. By 1876, Spain and France had divided all Basque lands.

The dictator General Francisco Franco, who ruled Spain from 1939 to 1975, banned the Basque language and culture. Spanish culture and language were forced on the Basque people. Across the country, the Spanish government killed, tortured, and imprisoned people for political and cultural beliefs that Spain's dictator was opposed to. Thousands of Basque people fled the country in exile.

By the 1950s, several Basque resistance groups formed, including the Euskadi Ta Askatasuna (ETA). The ETA's founders believed that other Basque nationalist groups were too passive in their resistance to Franco's dictatorship. They turned to violent action to get their message heard. At first, many people supported the ETA in its fight against the Franco government.

Since its creation, the ETA has caused more than 800 deaths, wounded hundreds of people, kidnapped multiple people, and carried out bombings, robberies, and other acts of sabotage. It has targeted various members of the Spanish community, including political representatives, security forces, businessmen, judges, journalists, and educators.

WHY TERRORISM?

While the specific causes of terrorism might differ for each person or group, terrorism in general is a calculated choice. Terrorists use violent action to achieve short-term and long-term goals, such as spreading fear and affecting political change. The decision to use violent action is a complicated one, and experts believe it is influenced by many factors.

The Spanish government falsely accused ETA of carrying out the 2004 Madrid train bombings.

Many members of the ETA have died at the hands of military, police, and security forces. At different points in history, Spanish, British, French, and American authorities have called ETA a terrorist organization.

Basque support of ETA's terrorist methods has decreased since some Basque provinces gained their independence. Several times, the ETA has attempted unsuccessfully put an end to the violence. The ETA declared ceasefires in 1989, 1996, 1998, and 2006. Each ceasefire broke down after another violent attack. In January 2011, the ETA declared a permanent and general ceasefire.

Despite the latest ceasefire, ETA has stated that it will not stop working to achieve an independent Basque state. Instead of terrorism, it says that the group plans to use other methods to achieve its independence goal. However, according to French police, several ETA members are reportedly still stockpiling weapons and explosives.

What do you think? Is the ETA a terrorist group? Would it have become violent if violence hadn't been thrust upon it first by the Franco government?

RELIGION

Conflict between religions can also cause people to choose violent action. Members of a particular religious group might want to overthrow a secular government and establish a state governed by the laws of their religion. They could feel discriminated against and oppressed. They may believe their religion and beliefs are under attack from outsiders.

While not every religious extremist is violent, some believe that terrorism is the best way to achieve their goals. In some cases, religious extremists choose terrorism as a way to battle people and groups that they view as enemies of their religion.

IMPACT FACT

Chechen terrorist organizations are an example of ethno-nationalists. They have attacked the government and people of Russia in the attempt to form their own state.

A LITTLE INDEPENDENCE

In 1980, three of the four Spanish Basque provinces unified as the Basque Autonomous Community. They were granted limited autonomy, recognition of their culture and language, and control of their schools and police. Although some members of the Basque community were pleased with these gains, some hardline members of the ETA continued to fight for full independence for the Basque people.

THE ZEALOTS

IMPACT FACT

The Zealots were known to the Romans as *sicarii* or dagger-men.

Throughout history, terrorism has been used by Christians, Jews, Hindus, Muslims, and others as a tactic for change. More than 2,000 years ago, the first acts of terrorism were performed by religious fanatics. One example occurred around 66 to 73 CE, when a Jewish sect called the Zealots fought against the Roman Empire's occupation of the land that is now known as Israel.

The Zealots carried out a campaign of frightening public assassinations to send a compelling message to the Romans and their sympathizers. In the middle of a crowded marketplace, a Zealot would emerge and draw a primitive dagger called a sica that was hidden in his robes. In view of all present, he would violently slit the throat of a Roman legionnaire or a Jewish person who had been judged a traitor by the Zealots. This public act of violence was intended to send a powerful message to the Romans and the Jews who cooperated with them. The Zealots were also reported to have poisoned granaries used by the Romans and sabotaged the area's water supply.[1]

This panel from the Arch of Titus shows Romans returning from a Jerusalem temple with items they stole. The Zealots reacted to the Roman occupation with terrorist activities.

credit: steerpike

THE JEWISH DEFENSE LEAGUE

A more recent example of terrorism linked to religion can be found with the Jewish Defense League (JDL). Founded in 1968 in New York City, the JDL is a radical group that preaches violent anti-Arab, Jewish nationalism. Its roots began in the racial tensions that occurred between the mostly Jewish teachers union and African-American residents during the New York City teachers union strikes in 1968. JDL followers are influenced by the words of the group's late founder, Rabbi Meir Kahane, who preached that Jews face fierce anti-Semitism and must protect themselves by any means, even violence.

Kahane wrote for an Orthodox Jewish periodical called *The Jewish Weekly*. He filled the publication with stories of African-Americans and Puerto Ricans terrorizing Jewish people in Manhattan. JDL units patrolling Jewish sections of neighborhoods alienated other ethnic groups. Kahane also took an aggressive anti-Arab stand. The JDL calls for the removal of all Arabs from Israel.

The group's members have carried out many terrorist attacks in the United States and around the world, especially against Palestinians living in the Middle East's West Bank. In 1994, a JDL member named Baruch Goldstein murdered 29 Palestinian Muslims as they knelt in prayer at a mosque in Hebron, a Palestinian city in the West Bank.

Terrorism sparked by religious motives is often more violent and causes greater fatalities and casualties than other types of terrorism. Some of the most brutal terrorist attacks in the past 30 years have been linked to people with religious motives.

Why is religious terrorism more deadly?

TERROR FOR SOVIET JEWS

In the 1970s, the JDL switched its focus to the struggle of Jews in the Soviet Union. By terrorizing Soviet establishments in the United States, the group attempted to pressure the Soviet Union to lift its ban on emigration to Israel and other anti-Semitic policies. JDL attacks included pouring blood over the head of a Soviet diplomat in Washington, DC, and planting a smoke bomb at Carnegie Hall during a Soviet orchestra performance. Many Jewish people in Moscow, however, did not support the JDL's actions in the United States. They feared it would hurt their cause and give Soviet officials an excuse to pass even more anti-Semitic policies.

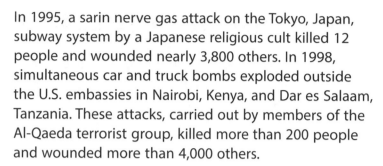
According to a global think tank called Institute for Economics and Peace, four known terrorist groups—Islamic State/ISIS, Boko Haram, the Taliban, and Al-Qaeda—were responsible for 74 percent of all deaths from terrorism in 2015.[2] All four groups are classified as religious terrorist organizations.

Derogatory names, such as "dogs" or "children of Satan," portray the terrorists' victims as less than human or unworthy of living.

In 1995, a sarin nerve gas attack on the Tokyo, Japan, subway system by a Japanese religious cult killed 12 people and wounded nearly 3,800 others. In 1998, simultaneous car and truck bombs exploded outside the U.S. embassies in Nairobi, Kenya, and Dar es Salaam, Tanzania. These attacks, carried out by members of the Al-Qaeda terrorist group, killed more than 200 people and wounded more than 4,000 others.

For the religious terrorist, violence is a sacramental act, or divine duty performed on God's command. They believe their violent acts are not immoral, but instead are morally justified and necessary to meet God's will. Religion, through sacred texts and clerical authorities, becomes a way to justify the violence. For this reason, clerics and other religious figures often bless, or sanction, terrorist operations before they begin.

While non-religious terrorists often view violence as a way to fix a system or create a new system, religious terrorists often see themselves as outsiders working for fundamental changes in existing society.

Religious terrorists often have a sense of isolation from the rest of the world, and a broader, more open-ended definition of enemies that can be targets. In fact, they often dehumanize enemies, calling them infidels, dogs, and children of Satan. In combination, these views allow religious terrorists to carry out the most destructive and deadly attacks.

In the late twentieth century, religious terrorism has become a significant player on the global stage of terrorism. Religious-motivated terror attacks have increased in frequency, size, and violence around the world.

ISLAMIC EXTREMISTS

In the modern era, Islamic extremists are some of the world's most well-known religious terrorists. Terrorist groups such as the Islamic State, the Taliban, and Al-Qaeda follow Islamic fundamentalist beliefs. Islamic fundamentalism is a movement within several Muslim nations. Fundamentalists believe in a literal interpretation of Islam's holy book, the Qur'an. They believe that Muslims must strictly follow the religious practices and moral codes found in the Qur'an.

For these people, Islamic religious law is the only law, and there is no separation between religious and political life. Therefore, they seek to institute Islamic law, including strict codes of behavior, for all citizens. In their view, the only legitimate governments are those that adopt Islamic law.

Many Islamic fundamentalists see the world in black and white—either a person is one of them or stands against them. This view affects how they interact with members of other faiths, including other Muslims, Christians, Jews, and Hindus. They strongly oppose "corrupting" secular and Western influences and strive to eliminate them. While most Islamic fundamentalists are not violent, some extremists believe that violence is necessary to achieve the worldwide spread of Islamic law.

Islamic extremists represent a small minority of Muslims. The majority of the world's Muslim people openly reject Islamic extremism.

ISLAMIC CODES OF BEHAVIOR

For millions of people worldwide, Islam is more than a religion; it is a way of life. Islam's sacred text, the Qur'an, gives instructions to Muslims on how to conduct themselves in all areas of life. The Qur'an provides guidance on worship, politics, marriage, family life, care for the poor, hygiene, community, and economics. The Sunna is a body of Islamic customs and practices based on the prophet Muhammad's words and deeds. After the death of Muhammad, the Muslim community established a set of laws based on the Qur'an and the Sunna. This Islamic law, known as the Shari'a, applies to all individual and community activities. Shari'a law provides the rules for living a righteous life.

In the late 1970s, Islamic extremism surged in Iran and other places in the Middle East when an uprising in Iran toppled the nation's pro-Western monarchy and replaced it with an anti-Western Islamic republic in 1979. The new Iranian leaders were Islamic extremists. At the time, they sought to spread their religious views to other Middle Eastern nations and replace moderate governments with Islamic republics. In the years since 1979, Iran's leaders have been accused of funding and providing support for numerous terrorist groups that carry out anti-Western attacks, including Hezbollah in Lebanon.

> Today, Islamic extremists blame Western influences, particularly the United States, for interfering in the Middle East.

They view Western culture as a corrupting influence on Muslims. In addition, they oppose the presence of American and other Western military troops in the Middle East. Islamic extremists also believe that Israel occupies lands that rightfully belong to the Palestinian people. They blame the United States for its support of Israel and the Israeli struggle against the Palestinians.

HEZBOLLAH

Formed in 1982 after the Israeli invasion of Lebanon, Hezbollah is an Islamic militant group and political party. Its name means the "Party of God." The group supports the spread of the Shi'a branch of Islam around the world, and perceives its fighting as self-defense and its actions as sanctioned by God.

According to Sheikh Muhammed Hussein Fadlallah, who has been said to have inspired Hezbollah's leaders, Israel's invasion of Lebanon was a symbol of the West's hostility toward Islam. America was seen as the root cause of problems in the Middle East, through its support of Israel in the region. According to one Islamic cleric, Hezbollah's struggle against Israel's occupation of Lebanon is not led by military commanders. Instead, it is directed by the tenets of Islam.

To carry out its divine resistance, Hezbollah has been involved in many anti-American and anti-Western terrorist attacks. The group is linked to the 1983 attacks on the U.S. embassy and U.S. Marines barracks in Beirut, as well as the hijacking of TWA Flight 847 in 1985 and the 1996 attack on the Khobar Towers in Saudi Arabia. Hezbollah has also focused some of its attacks on Israel and its interests. In July 2012, Hezbollah members exploded a bomb on a bus in Bulgaria, killing five Israeli tourists and a Bulgarian citizen.

President and Mrs. Reagan honor the victims of the bombing of the U.S. embassy in Beirut, Lebanon, by the group Hezbollah.

credit: National Archive

The U.S. embassy in Beirut after being attacked with a car bomb in 1983

credit: U.S. Army

> **The primary goal of Hamas is to create a Palestinian state and to destroy Israel through holy war called jihad.**

HAMAS

Another example of an Islamic fundamentalist organization that has turned to terrorism is Hamas. Formed in 1987, Harakat al-Muqawama al-Islamiya, better known as Hamas, operates in the West Bank and Gaza in the Middle East.

The Arabic word *hamas* means "zeal" or "enthusiasm." Sections of Hamas are dedicated to religious, military, political, and security operations. It also runs a social welfare program and operates schools, hospitals, and religious institutions.

> Hamas's ultimate goal is to establish an Islamic fundamentalist Palestinian state.

IMPACT FACT

Since Israel's withdrawal from the Gaza Strip in 2005, Hamas and other Palestinian terrorist organizations have fired more than 11,000 rockets into Israel.

To achieve its goals, the Hamas founding charter called for jihad, or holy war, against Israel. Hamas's religious war against all Jewish people was made clear by a sermon preached in 1987 by Hamas's founder and spiritual leader, Imam Sheikh Ahmad Ibrahim Yassin. He declared, "Six million descendants of monkeys now rule in all the nations of the world, but their day, too, will come. Allah! Kill them all, do not leave even one."[3]

Hamas's military branch is known as the Izz al-Din al-Qassam Brigades. This branch has carried out many anti-Israel attacks, including bombings against civilians, small-arms attacks, roadside explosions, and rocket attacks. Since 1993, Hamas is believed to have killed more than 500 people in more than 350 terrorist attacks, according to the Council on Foreign Relations.

In Palestine's 2006 elections, Hamas won a majority of seats in the Palestinian Legislative Council. In recent years, Hamas leaders have expressed an interest in a truce and living in a Palestinian state side-by-side with Israel. Even so, some countries, such as the United States, Britain, and Canada, have designated Hamas as a foreign terrorist organization. Other countries, such as Russia, Norway, and Switzerland, do not consider it to be a terrorist organization. Do countries have different reasons for labeling a group as a terrorist? How might that change political relationships between countries?

AL-QAEDA

One of the most well-known Islamic fundamentalist terror groups is Al-Qaeda. Founded by Osama bin Laden, the Al-Qaeda network's goal is to promote Islamic fundamentalism.

From the start, bin Laden has framed Al-Qaeda's mission in religious terms. Years before the September 11, 2001, attacks on the United States, bin Laden declared a religious war on the United States. He released two declarations in the form of fatwas, a type of Islamic religious decree, in 1996 and 1998. In his first fatwa, bin Laden presented his view that Islam was under attack and he and other Muslims were reluctant defenders with no option but to embrace violence to respond to an aggressive enemy. He ended the fatwa with the following call to battle for Muslims around the world.

> "Your brothers in Palestine and in the land of the two Holy Places are calling upon your help and asking you to take part in fighting against the enemy your enemy and their enemy the Americans and the Israelis. They are asking you to do whatever you can, with one ['s] own means and ability, to expel the enemy, humiliated and defeated, out of the sanctities of Islam."[4]

FATAH

Fatah and Hamas are the two main political groups for Palestine. A powerful political movement, Fatah is the largest member of the Palestinian Liberation Organization (PLO) and controls the Palestinian Authority (PA), which runs the West Bank. While both organizations share the goal of creating a Palestinian state, they differ on how to achieve their goal. While Hamas has refused to renounce violence against Israel, Fatah has renounced violence and recognized Israel as part of peace efforts in the region.

The second fatwa, which was signed by bin Laden and four other Islamic religious leaders, carried much of the same message. It explained that the sins of the Americans were a clear declaration of war on God, his messenger, and Muslims. It declared the following.

> "The ruling to kill the Americans and their allies—civilians and military—is an individual duty for every Muslim who can do it in any country in which it is possible to do it . . . . [E]very Muslim who believes in God and wishes to be rewarded to comply with God's order to kill the Americans and plunder their money wherever and whenever they find it."[5]

Six months after the release of the second fatwa, suicide bombers carried out the simultaneous attacks on the U.S. embassies in Kenya and Tanzania. Al-Qaeda members also carried out an attack that damaged the U.S. Navy warship USS *Cole* while it was in harbor at Aden, Yemen, in 2000.

The attack on the USS *Cole* killed 17 U.S. sailors and injured 39 others.

And on September 11, 2001, Al-Qaeda carried out the deadliest terrorist attack on American soil. It used passenger airplanes to attack the World Trade Center in New York City and the Pentagon near Washington, DC. A fourth plane crashed in the Pennsylvania countryside before it could reach its intended target.

Although American attacks on Al-Qaeda bases in Afghanistan after 9/11 have hurt the organization's ability to plan and execute large-scale terrorist attacks, the group continues to operate. Al-Qaeda terrorists still plan and carry out attacks in many countries throughout Asia, Africa, and the Middle East.

The word *Al-Qaeda* is Arabic for "the Base."

IMPACT FACT

On September 11, 2001, the passengers of United Flight 93 rushed the cockpit and prevented the hijackers from reaching their intended target, the U.S. Capitol, before the plane crashed in Pennsylvania.

A MIX OF MOTIVATIONS

Sometimes, a terrorist organization has both ethno-nationalist and religious motivations. The Palestine Liberation Organization (PLO) was founded in 1964 with the goal of establishing a Palestinian state on land currently held by the state of Israel. The PLO formed a number of terrorist organizations that carried out many violent attacks against Israel.

After years of violence, PLO leader Yasser Arafat signed a peace agreement with Israel in 1993. In the agreement, the Palestinians were granted limited self-government within the West Bank and Gaza Strip. The PLO agreed to stop its terrorist attacks. However, other terrorist groups in the region, such as Hamas, continued their attacks on Israeli targets.

> The statehood promised to Palestine in the peace agreement did not materialize, and the fight between Palestine and Israel continues to this day.

In Great Britain, the Provisional Irish Republican Army (IRA) is another group motivated by a mix of nationalism and religion. Formed in 1968, the IRA's goal was to end British rule in Northern Ireland and reunify all of Ireland as a Roman Catholic country. Protestants in Northern Ireland opposed the group and wanted to remain part of Britain.

IMPACT FACT

Throughout history, the Gaza Strip has been controlled by many different peoples and empires, including the Ottoman Empire in the early sixteenth century, the British during World War I, Egypt, and Israel.

A mural in Belfast, bidding British soldiers "Safe Home"

credit: Jimmy Harris

For decades, the IRA attacked British military and police targets in Northern Ireland, as well as targets in England. In the 1990s, the IRA began to negotiate with the British government. In April 1998, they signed the Good Friday Agreement. The agreement created a new Northern Ireland Assembly made up of Roman Catholics and Protestants and promised greater cooperation between Northern Ireland and the southern Irish Republic. Under the agreement, all paramilitary groups were to disarm, including the IRA. At first the IRA refused, but eventually it complied.

By July 2006, the British and Irish governments certified that the Provisional IRA had ceased terrorist operations. However, since then, a splinter group that calls itself the Real Irish Republican Army has continued to carry out terrorist attacks against British targets in Northern Ireland, striking in 2015 and 2016. Do you think having more than one motivation might make people more likely to commit acts of terrorism? Why or why not?

POLITICAL MOTIVATIONS: LEFT-WING GROUPS

Some people are driven to terrorism because of intense political beliefs and a hatred of the people in power. Politically driven terrorists can usually be divided into two main groups: left wing and right wing.

Left-wing groups often support radical political or social reform. Inspired by communist thinkers such as Karl Marx (1818–1883), Vladimir Lenin (1870–1924), and Mao Zedong (1893–1976), they see capitalist economic systems as the main cause of poverty and inequality worldwide. They believe that revolution is needed to rebuild a more just society based on communism and socialist ideals.

For some groups that see themselves as repressed by a financial system, class, or government, violence is an attractive option. They believe they are fighting for the world's poor. In Peru, the Sendero Luminoso, or Shining Path, is a left-wing group founded in 1970. The group aimed to overthrow Peru's government and replace it with communism. Its first act of violence occurred in 1980, when members destroyed ballot boxes the night before the country's national elections.

During the next decade, the group carried out a series of bombings, assassinations, and other attacks against the state. It quickly became known for its brutality, even holding violent public executions by stoning. In July 1992, Shining Path members exploded a car bomb in Lima, killing 25 people and injuring dozens more.

The Shining Path has been officially designated a terrorist organization by governments throughout the world, including the United States and European Union. Since 2000, the group's membership has declined. Its attacks on targets have also decreased, as the remaining members have shifted their main focus to drug trafficking.

RIGHT-WING EXTREMISM

The opposite of left-wing groups, right-wing extremist groups do not want to bring about revolutionary change. Instead, they want to preserve the status quo and protect traditional ways of life. They perceive their values and lifestyle to be under attack from other groups. In addition, they often believe they are superior to others, which can lead to fear and hatred of people who are different from them. Some right-wing groups are motivated by fundamentalist Christian beliefs, while others are motivated by nationalism, racism, and sexism.

Right-wing extremists sometimes turn to terrorism to achieve their goals. With an uncompromising belief that they are superior—in terms of race, ethnicity, or gender—they can believe that violence is justified to protect the purity of the group. Violence becomes acceptable against people outside their group because they stand in the way of the group's goals. Xenophobia, an intense and irrational fear of people from other countries, causes extremists to oppose immigration and blame immigrants for a country's problems.

Right-wing extremists might attack foreigners or members of ethnic minorities.

Unpopular government policies can spark right-wing violence if extremists believe the policies threaten their traditional values and their group's supremacy. Tax policy, abortion rights, and alternative lifestyles have triggered violence from right-wing extremists in America.

Historically, right-wing terrorism has not been as well organized or focused as left-wing terrorist groups. Typically, many right-wing terrorists have worked in small groups or gangs to carry out random attacks. For example, racist skinheads in Europe often act alone or in small gangs to carry out hate crimes against minorities. These hate crimes have been random and spontaneous and not part of a coordinated campaign.

Terrorism affects people and countries worldwide. The people who become terrorists come from many different backgrounds and are motivated by a variety of causes and ideologies. As a result, there is no one, single portrait of a terrorist. What they do have in common, however, is that they all have decided that violence is the best way to achieve their goals.

KEY QUESTIONS

- Why do you think calling an enemy by a dehumanizing name makes it easier to cause more violence?

- Why is religion a motivating factor for terrorism? What is the connection between intense emotion and violence?

- What might be some solutions for ethno-nationalism and religious terrorism?

WHAT DOES TERRORISM LOOK LIKE?

People who commit acts of terrorism come from all backgrounds, nationalities, religions, and genders. They can be young or old, men or women.

- **Quickly draw a picture of what you think a typical terrorist looks like.** Compare your drawing with those of your classmates. What similarities are there? What differences do you notice? Discuss the following questions.

  - Why did you choose the features in your drawing?

  - Where do your ideas of what a terrorist looks like come from?

  - Do you think this idea represents a majority of terrorists around the world?

  - Do you think Americans have a stereotype of terrorists? Explain.

- **Now, using the Internet, look at the pictures of several well-known terrorists.**

  - Osama bin Laden

  - Ted Kaczynski

  - Eric Rudolph

  - Sally Jones

  - Martin McGuinness

  - Ahmed Ghailani

  - Assata Shakur

- **Do these people match your picture of a typical terrorist?** Why or why not? Compare and contrast them to the stereotypes you discussed earlier.

IMPACT FACT

A stereotype is the inaccurate belief that all people who share a physical or cultural trait are the same.

To investigate more, consider how having a stereotype of terrorism can be a problem in society. How do stereotypes affect Muslim communities and people of Middle Eastern descent in the United States? How would you feel if people assumed that you might be a terrorist because of the way you looked or your religion?

CONSIDER DIFFERENT VIEWPOINTS

For decades, there has been conflict between Israelis and Palestinians in the Middle East. The conflict stems from a dispute over land. Despite repeated attempts, there has been no lasting peace settlement between the two groups. Several terror groups have formed as a result of this conflict, including Hezbollah and Hamas.

* **You can explore these Internet sites to understand the background of the conflict between the Israelis and Palestinians.**

  🔍 BBC Profile of Israel

  🔍 Israeli-Palestinian conflict

* **You can also explore what life is like for people living in this region.**

  🔍 Life in a West Bank Settlement

  🔍 Life in a Palestinian Refugee Camp

* **Imagine that you are a Jewish teen living in a Jewish settlement in the West Bank.** What is your life like? How do you feel about the conflict between the Jews and Palestinians? How has it affected your life? How has terrorism affected you?

* **Compare the experience of a Jewish teen to that of a Palestinian teen living in a refugee camp in the West Bank.** How would your life be different from your Jewish neighbor's? How would it be the same? How has the conflict affected your life? How has terrorism affected you?

* **Create a chart.** Compare and contrast the lives and experiences of the Jewish and Palestinian teens.

To investigate more, put yourself in the shoes of one of these teens. Write a diary entry from either the Jewish or Palestinian teen's point of view. Make sure to use description and sensory details in your entry.

Chapter 3 ▶
Tactics and Targets

Who are the targets
of terrorist attacks?

WHAT'S THE MATTER?

I FEEL SICK WHEN I READ OF TERRORISTS ATTACKING CIVILIANS, EVEN LITTLE KIDS.

ME, TOO. IT'S LIKE THEY'RE TRYING TO MAKE YOU THINK NO ONE IS SAFE...

...AND THAT YOU SHOULD JUST STAY AT HOME AND STOP LIVING YOUR LIFE.

THAT'S EXACTLY IT!

THEY'RE TRYING TO SCARE EVERYBODY INTO DOING WHAT THEY WANT.

Terrorists choose their targets to cause as much physical and psychological damage and disruption as possible to achieve their goals of bringing about social and political change.

At approximately 9:20 p.m. on November 13, 2015, an explosion detonated outside Stade de France, a sports stadium in a northern Paris suburb in France. Inside the stadium, thousands of fans, including French President Francois Hollande, were watching France play Germany in a soccer match. A few minutes later, a second explosion blasted outside the stadium.

Across Paris, gunmen armed with assault rifles and explosives attacked at six locations, killing civilians. At one restaurant, a suicide bomber blew himself up, injuring several people nearby.

At 9:40 p.m., three attackers armed with assault weapons entered the nearby Bataclan concert hall during a performance of an American band and opened fire, killing 89 people. When the French police stormed the concert hall a few hours later, two attackers detonated suicide belt explosives, killing themselves before they could be arrested. The police shot and killed the third attacker.

The coordinated attacks killed 130 people and left hundreds more wounded. The next day, the terror group ISIS claimed responsibility for the attacks in an online statement.

To most people, terrorist attacks such as the one in Paris appear random and senseless. From the perspective of the terrorists, every detail of the attacks is carefully planned, from targets to tactics, to achieve very specific objectives. The targets chosen, the methods used, and the scale of the violence are typically selected with thought and care.

THE OBJECTIVE

Most terrorists plan their actions with a specific objective in mind. Often, this objective involves political or social change. The type of change a group seeks depends on the group and its motives. For example, ethno-nationalist terrorists might seek to gain human rights or form their own nation. Religious terrorists seek to bring a new faith-based order to society. Left-wing political terrorists may seek to destroy financial systems and replace them with communism-based systems.

Terrorists often plan attacks that will inflict the most psychological damage. In many terrorist attacks, the main impact is not the physical damage to a target, but the psychological impact on people. By attacking symbolic targets such as cultural symbols, political institutions, and public leaders, terrorists can spread fear and anxiety in many people.

Is Terrorism Effective?

Whether or not terrorism is effective depends on your perspective. From the terrorist's point of view, the effectiveness of an attack can be measured in different ways. Did it gain enough media attention? Did it get the attention of political parties and governments? Did the actions cause the target audience to change their attitudes or behaviors in a desired way? Did it disrupt a society's normal routines and spread fear among a community? All of these factors determine an attack's success from the terror group's point of view.

For example, after the 9/11 attacks in New York City, many New Yorkers and other Americans experienced symptoms of stress and anxiety. Jeanine Hoff was on a New York City subway when the two World Trade Center towers were attacked. When the subway trains stopped, Hoff made her way through the tunnels up to the streets. It took nearly eight hours before she found out that her husband, who worked in Lower Manhattan, was safe. A few days later while eating breakfast, she began having trouble breathing.

"I thought I had eaten too much or was having a sugar rush. I became dizzy, had tunnel-vision and severe chest pains. I didn't know what was wrong and as the minutes passed, it became progressively worse . . . . Several days later, it happened again. The dizziness was unbearable and I was gasping for air. I had to leave the subway and return to the hospital."[2]

Eventually, doctors diagnosed Hoff with panic attacks. The fear affected her life in several ways. She stopped flying, driving, and riding the subway. She avoided anything unknown and struggled with anxiety and depression. Eventually, Hoff and her husband left New York to build a new life in Florida.

Terrorists also plan specific actions to disrupt the normal routines of a community. By doing so, they demonstrate a government's inability to protect its citizens, which can weaken popular support for leaders. For example, bombings on public transportation systems can have a significant effect on a community's normal routines. In 2005, four suicide bombers with backpacks full of explosives attacked London, England, killing more than 50 people and injuring hundreds more.

The attackers carried out coordinated attacks, detonating three explosives on the subway and one on a double-decker bus and disrupting the London public transportation system. It was the worst single terrorist attack on British soil.[3] Why do terrorist actions such as this weaken a population's confidence in the government?

Terrorists also carefully plan attacks to bring awareness to their cause. When an attack is successful, it can generate enormous attention from communities, governments, and other interests. Television, the Internet, and social media can bring the news of a terror attack and its devastating effects into the homes of millions of people around the world in only a few seconds. News stations interrupt regular programming to broadcast live video and audio from terrorist attacks. News reporters interview witnesses and terrorism experts live on air, increasing media coverage of the event.

Some terrorists plan their actions to inspire other citizens to join their revolutionary cause. For many terrorists, each action creates propaganda that can most effectively create a revolutionary environment.

> For example, they might choose to bomb a government troop transport truck, believing that the action will cause the government to overreact against the community.

The extremists can then point to government actions as yet another example of the state's repression. They can argue that the people need to join into a rebellion against their repressive leaders.

AL-QAEDA'S TERRORIST MANUAL

In May 2000, police found a document written in Arabic in the home of an alleged Al-Qaeda member in Manchester, England. Approximately 180 pages, the document was titled *Military Studies in the Jihad Against the Tyrants*. It was an operation manual with detailed instructions for how operatives should engage in cell-based terrorist activities in foreign countries. The manual included required missions, such as gathering information about the enemy, kidnapping enemy personnel, and assassinating enemy personnel as well as foreign tourists. It listed security steps the operatives should take, including keeping fake identity cards and passports and taking identification photographs without a beard. The manual also instructed married operatives not to talk to their wives about jihad matters.

A SPECIFIC AUDIENCE

Many terrorists plan their actions with a specific audience in mind. Who are they trying to reach and why? Capturing the attention of a specific audience enables the terrorists to better spread their message and achieve their goals. For example, terrorists might plan an action to attract the attention of people who are indifferent to their cause. This could force these people to end their indifference and motivate them to join the movement for change. Other times, the intended audience is a government and its allies, to force them to acknowledge and respond to citizens' demands.

Another audience could include potential and existing supporters. Some terrorist actions are planned to motivate a large group of people to join and support a revolutionary cause.

CHOOSING A TARGET

Terrorists choose their targets with careful deliberation. Targets are rarely selected because of military value, such as disrupting supply or communication lines. These disruptions are usually easily fixed or solved. Instead, terrorists typically choose targets that have symbolic value or will receive the most media coverage.

Not only can an attack on the right target cause the enemy significant damage, it can also create propaganda that attracts supporters to the extremists' cause or sends a message to a larger audience. High-profile, sentimental, and significant targets are often chosen. These include embassies, diplomatic personnel, international symbols, symbolic buildings, symbolic people, and passenger carriers with large numbers of civilians. Attacks on these targets generate graphic media images that can be spread across television screens, the Internet, and newspapers.

METHODS OF ATTACK

With an objective, target, and audience in mind, terrorist groups plan specific actions. The methods they use vary by group, situation, and objectives, but they are almost always extremely calculated. Some groups carry out attacks using suicide bombings, while other groups prefer arson or kidnappings. Some of the most commonly used tactics include bombings, sidearm assaults, kidnappings, and hijackings.

Bombings are a common method of attack because they allow terrorists to inflict significant physical and psychological damage on a target or community. Sidearm attacks using pistols and rifles are other common methods to ambush, assassinate, or inflict casualties on a target. Kidnappings can be used to extort money for ransom or to create propaganda. In some cases, the kidnappers execute the hostages to send a message.

> Hijacking passenger planes, boats, or other large vehicles can create many casualties and trigger terror across a large population.

In some cases, a particular method becomes a signature of a specific terrorist group. For example, a maneuver called kneecapping is a known tactic of the Irish Republican Army, Irish Protestant loyalists, and Italy's Red Brigades. Other groups, such as Abu Sayyaf in the Philippines, use kidnappings as their signature method, while still others, such as Iraqi insurgents, are known for suicide bombing attacks.

SYMBOLIC TARGETS

The targets selected by Al-Qaeda for the September 11 attacks were highly symbolic. The World Trade Center represented the American and Western economy and the Pentagon represents the American military. Attacks against these targets did little to disrupt the U.S. military, but they generated worldwide media attention and fear.

WEAPONS OF CHOICE

Historically, firearms and explosives have been the weapons of choice for many terrorists. Small firearms and handheld weapons have been and continue to be some of the most common weapons used by terrorists. Typical firearms include submachine guns, assault rifles, and rocket-propelled grenades. Less commonly used by terrorists but still very effective, precision-guided munitions are weapons that can be guided to a target by infrared or other tracking technologies.

Terrorists also frequently use explosives to attack symbolic targets. Most terrorist bombs are homemade, improvised weapons instead of factory-manufactured bombs.

The homemade bombs are often made from explosives that are readily available, such as dynamite and TNT.

Some explosives are as simple as a gasoline-filled bottle with a flaming rag for a trigger. Other bombs are made with plastic explosives, which include compounds such as RDX, Semtex, or Composite-4. Plastic explosives have a putty-like texture, which makes them easy to mold.

Bombs can use explosives made from common ammonium nitrate fertilizers soaked in fuel oil. This type of bomb is often used in car or truck bombs. In April 1995, American terrorist Timothy McVeigh loaded a 2-ton bomb made from ANFO explosives into a truck. McVeigh parked the deadly truck outside the Alfred P. Murrah Federal Building in Oklahoma City. When it exploded, the truck bomb destroyed the federal building and killed 168 people, including 19 children.

Afghan Islamic warriors have used the American-made Stinger, a shoulder-fired, surface-to-air missile with an infrared targeting system, to shoot Soviet helicopters and other aircraft.

A car bomb explodes in South Baghdad, Iraq, in 2005

credit: SPC Ronald Shaw Jr., U.S. Army

Large amounts of explosives can be loaded into cars and trucks. Vehicle bombs blend easily into crowded city streets, making it hard for law enforcement to identify the threat. Easy to make, vehicle bombs have been used many times by terrorist groups around the world. In August 1998, a car bomb exploded in Omagh, Northern Ireland, killing 29 people and injuring more than 220 more. The Real Irish Republican Army claimed responsibility for the attack.

Many terrorists put explosives into ordinary pipes and cap the ends to make a pipe bomb. Sometimes, nuts, nails, and other shrapnel are attached to the pipe bomb to inflict more damage when it explodes. In the United States, pipe bombs have been used in several abortion clinic bombings and at the 1996 Summer Olympics in Atlanta, Georgia.

IMPACT FACT

In 2005, Dhari Ali al-Fayadh, a member of Iraq's parliament, was assassinated by a suicide car bomb.

WEAPONS OF MASS DESTRUCTION

Some weapons can cause mass devastation and high numbers of casualties. For terrorists who have the goal of killing as many people as possible, these weapons of mass destruction (WMDs), hold a particular interest. WMDs include biological agents, chemical agents, radiological agents, and nuclear weapons.

Biological agents are weapons created from living organisms that cause disease or death. Some viruses, fungi, and bacteria can be used to make biological weapons. Toxins such as botulism can be used to poison the food or water supply. Experts agree that the most likely biological agents that could be weaponized and used by terrorists include anthrax, the smallpox virus, and botulinum toxin. The bubonic plague is a bacterium that is highly infectious and often fatal.

The first case of widespread use of a biological agent for attack occurred days after the September 11 attacks in 2001. Letters containing anthrax spores arrived at several news media offices and U.S. senators' offices. Anthrax is a disease that affects livestock and humans. It exists as spores or can be suspended in an aerosol. Humans can become sick when exposed to anthrax through contact with cuts in the skin or by eating contaminated meat.

In the 2001 anthrax attack, five Americans were killed and 17 developed anthrax poisoning. Mass panic erupted, as many people across the country feared that a deadly weapon could arrive in the mail at any time. Post offices that handled the infected mail closed. After a long investigation, the FBI concluded that Dr. Bruce Ivins, an American microbiologist, was the likely terrorist. Dr. Ivins committed suicide in 2008, hours before he was to be indicted for the crime.

Chemical agents are chemical substances that can be turned into weapons that cause disease or death. Chemical agents come in gas, liquid, or solid form. Some chemical agents, such as pesticides, are easily purchased. Others can be manufactured by extremists. Examples of potential weaponized chemical agents include phosgene gas, chlorine gas, mustard gas, and various nerve gases. A single drop of certain nerve gases, such as sarin, tabun, and VX, can block nerve messages in the body.

In 2013, surface-to-surface rockets delivered the nerve agent sarin to the suburbs of Damascus, Syria's capital city. At the time, the Syrian government was caught up in a civil war against rebels. After an investigation, the United Nations and several other countries concluded that the Syrian government had released the chemical attack on its own citizens. According to eyewitness and survivor accounts, after the rocket explosions, victims quickly experienced symptoms such as shortness of breath, disorientation, eye irritation, blurred vision, nausea, vomiting, and weakness. Many lost consciousness. First responders to the area reported seeing many people, including children, lying on the ground either dead or unconscious.

Radiological agents emit radiation that can harm living organisms. Typically, these agents must be ingested, inhaled, or absorbed through the skin in order to cause harm. Although this type of WMD has not been used in a terror attack yet, terrorism experts believe that radioactive elements could be placed in a dirty bomb and detonated in a civilian area. Without large quantities of radioactive materials, this type of bomb would most likely do little damage outside the initial blast area, but could have significant, disruptive, psychological effects on the people.

Nuclear weapons are another WMD threat. An explosion from a nuclear bomb would devastate the immediate blast area and send deadly radiation to an area surrounding the blast zone.

SURVIVOR'S STORY: SARIN ATTACK

Kassem Eid was a Syrian citizen who survived the 2013 sarin nerve gas attack. In an article he wrote for *The New York Times*, he remembers that night.

"On Aug. 21, 2013, I woke up in the dark around 4:45 a.m., struggling to breathe. My eyes were burning, my head was throbbing, and my throat was blocked. I was suffocating.

I tried to inhale but all I heard was a horrible rasping sound as my throat closed up. My heart seemed about to explode.

Suddenly, my windpipe opened. A gust of air pierced my lungs. Needles seemed to stab my eyes. A searing pain clawed at my stomach. I doubled over and shouted to my roommates: 'Wake up! It's a chemical attack!'"[4]

You can read the rest of Kassem Eid's account of the chemical attack here.

 NYT Kassem Eid

In February 2002, Islamic terrorists recorded a video of the beheading of Daniel Pearl, an American citizen being held hostage. Since that first beheading video, several Islamic terror groups have released similar videos on the Internet that show the graphic beheading deaths of hostages. While some Islamic scholars have denounced these videos as against Islamic law, they have become popular with certain terror groups, including the Islamic State/ISIS. British and American aid workers, Japanese and American journalists, Kurdish and Syrian soldiers, and others have all been gruesomely beheaded for the camera, with the videos of their deaths being uploaded to the Internet as propaganda for a global audience. Some terror experts believe that while most people are repelled by the videos, they could attract sympathizers by projecting a god-like power.

It could also send radioactive debris into the atmosphere, which falls back to Earth as toxic fallout.

Although it is possible for terrorist groups to build their own large-scale nuclear weapon, it is an extremely technical and difficult process. Therefore, most terrorism experts believe that a more likely approach would be for terrorists to use smaller, more compact nuclear weapons.

SUICIDE BOMBERS

For many extremist groups, the use of a suicide bomber has become an accepted practice. A suicide bomber detonates a bomb, knowing that they will be killed in the explosion. The Tamil Tigers in Sri Lanka, Hezbollah in Lebanon, Al-Qaeda, and several Islamic insurgent groups use suicide bombers regularly. Suicide bombers have several distinct advantages over stationary bombs.

A human carrying a hidden bomb is less likely to attract attention and suspicion. They can move intelligently and react fluidly as conditions around them change. This type of bombing can also cause significant physical damage, loss of life, and psychological damage to an enemy.

For many terror groups, the loss of one member's life is an acceptable tradeoff for the damage they can cause. Some religious groups even believe that suicide bombers are martyrs and will be blessed by God in the afterlife. Suicide bombers are less expensive than other terrorism methods, partly because there's no need for an escape plan for the terrorist. Al-Qaeda and other Islamic extremist groups have sent suicide bombers to attack Western interests and other enemies.

In December 2009, a suicide bomber detonated an explosive-filled vest and killed himself, seven American Central Intelligence Agency (CIA) officials and contractors, a Jordanian intelligence officer, and an Afghan working for the CIA. The attack took place at a CIA base in Afghanistan. Several others were wounded in the explosion. The attacker was a Jordanian doctor who was operating as an Al-Qaeda double agent.

In April 2017, suicide bombers entered two churches in Egypt where worshippers had gathered for Palm Sunday services at the start of Holy Week leading up to the Easter holiday. The Islamic State group claimed responsibility for the attack, which killed 44 people and injured many more. In response to the attack, Egyptian President Abdel Fattah el-Sisi called for a three-month state of emergency.[5]

Soldiers take part in training exercises and work on detaining a suicide bomber

credit: SPC Tristan Bolden, Department of Defense

ONLINE DONATIONS

Terrorist organizations use the Internet to finance their activities. The Internet allows donors and the terrorist organizations to be anonymous in their transactions. Transferring funds through electronic payment services such as PayPal has become common and can even be completed on a cell phone. Online charities are another way for terrorist organizations to raise money. Some are existing organizations that terrorists have infiltrated, stealing money away from legitimate causes. Others hide their true intent behind vague mission statements, such as saying their fundraising is for humanitarian purposes.

CYBERTERRORISM

As governments and countries increasingly rely on digital technology and the Internet for daily functioning, the Internet has become a target. Cyberterrorism includes hacking into computer systems, spreading viruses, bringing websites offline, and making online threats. By disrupting the functioning of the Internet or bringing it offline, cyberterrorists can paralyze and disrupt governments, corporations, and other organizations.

In addition, the Internet has become a new tool for terrorists to communicate and recruit new members. On the Internet, terrorists can connect, plan, and execute attacks. According to the FBI, terror groups are also using the Internet to recruit and incite terrorism. Terror group websites promote violence and post videos on how to build bombs and weapons. They log onto social networks to share ideas and coordinate attacks.

Terrorism affects many different countries all around the world. In the next chapter, we'll take a look at the terrorism that has erupted on U.S. soil and examine the effect it has had on the U.S. population.

KEY QUESTIONS

- Why is psychological damage sometimes more harmful to a populace than physical damage?
- What role can the Internet play in preventing terrorist attacks?
- Why do we invent the kind of weapons that can cause widespread harm?

ASSASSINATIONS—AN ACT OF TERROR?

Throughout history, assassination is one tactic used by terror groups to achieve certain goals. However, not every assassination is an act of terror. When should murders of political figures be considered acts of terror or when are they simply horrible crimes? What separates terrorism from criminal activity?

* **Choose a political leader who was assassinated or who survived an assassination attempt.** Some leaders to consider researching include:

  * Abraham Lincoln

  * William McKinley

  * Czar Alexander II of Russia

  * Indira Gandhi

  * Benazir Bhutto

* **Research the assassination attempt on your chosen leader.** Consider the following questions.

  * Who was the leader? Where were they from? What country did they lead?

  * What political or social views did the leader have that were controversial?

  * Who was the perpetrator?

  * What was the perpetrator's objective? Did they succeed?

  * Did their actions affect history in the short-term? In the long-term?

  * Was the assassination attempt an act of terror? Explain your point of view.

> **To investigate more,** consider the question: Is assassination ever justified? Write a persuasive essay explaining your point of view on the issue.

ANALYSIS OF A TERROR ATTACK

Throughout history, many groups have used terrorism around the world to achieve their goals. Islamic extremists, including Al-Qaeda, are only one type of terror group within a larger population. Terrorists can be domestic or international. They have different views, objectives, targets, and tactics. Even within Islamic terror groups, motives and methods can be very different.

- **Choose two terror attacks carried out by different groups.** Using the Internet, research the details of each attack and prepare a narrative essay about the attack. Include details about the terrorists, their motivations, methods, targets, casualties, and damage. What was the response to and repercussions of the attack? Consider the following questions in your research.

  - What did the terrorists hope to achieve through violence?

  - Who or what did they target? Why?

  - What was the response to the attack?

  - How did other nations around the world respond?

  - Were the terrorists successful in achieving their goals? Explain.

- **After you have analyzed both attacks, compare and contrast them.** How were the attacks similar? How were they different? How did they compare in scope, participants, casualties, outcomes, etc.? What defines a "successful" terrorist attack? Was one attack considered more successful than the other? Why or why not?

> **To investigate more,** compare two terror attacks that occurred before and after 9/11. How did 9/11 change the way Islamic extremists carried out terror attacks? Explain your reasoning.

Chapter 4 ▶

Terrorism in the United States

Why do people in the United States turn to terrorism to reach their goals?

Some groups and individuals in the United States believe that the most effective way to get attention and work toward their goals is through violence.

In June 2015, a young white supremacist named Dylann Roof entered an African-American church in Charleston, South Carolina. He opened fire on parishioners who had gathered for Bible study, killing nine people and injuring one. All were African Americans. Roof later confessed that he committed the shooting in hopes of starting a race war in America. In 2017, a jury sentenced Roof to death.

The Charleston shooting is just one example of terrorism in the United States. Throughout the country's history, some people have turned to violence in support of their beliefs. Individuals and groups from every religious, ethnic, and political background, from the Ku Klux Klan in the southern United States to eco-terrorists in Oregon, have been involved in terrorist attacks in the United States.

Often, these people and groups have not been able to reach their goals of political or social change through traditional, nonviolent methods. As a result, they have turned to violent terrorism.

HOMEGROWN ISLAMIC EXTREMISTS

Because the September 11 attacks were carried out by terrorists born in the Middle East, many Americans believe that terrorism in the United States is primarily carried out by foreigners. However, many of the terror attacks in America since 9/11 have been carried out by American citizens or legal permanent residents, such as Nidal Hasan, the U.S. Army major who killed 13 people at Fort Hood, Texas, in 2009 and the Tsarnaev brothers, who carried out the 2013 Boston Marathon bombings.

> In some cases, citizens of the United States and other Western countries travel to the Middle East to terror camps for training.

Then, they return to their home countries to carry out terrorist attacks. Other times, American-born extremists get instructions and plan attacks from their homes, using the Internet. Before his attack on Fort Hood, Hasan was in frequent email contact with a militant Islamic cleric in Yemen. Often, extremists carry out their attacks alone or in pairs.

In June 2016, American-born Omar Mateen gunned down 49 people at a nightclub in Orlando, Florida, where much of the clientele identified as homosexual. It was the deadliest mass shooting in the United States and the deadliest terror attack since September 11, 2001.

KEEP ON RUNNING

After the Boston Marathon bombings in 2013, races from marathons to 5K charity events around the United States experienced a surge in registrations. To show their support and solidarity with the victims of the Boston bombings, people signed up to run, sometimes in record numbers. One of those people was Sherry Betts, a school counselor and avid runner from Leander, Texas. After the bombings, Betts registered for the Myles Standish Marathon in Plymouth, Massachusetts. She said running in the marathon was her way of showing that she was not afraid and terrorism had not changed the way she lived her life.

Mateen, who had pledged allegiance to the Islamic terror group ISIS, had been interviewed by the FBI in 2013 and 2014, but was not thought to be a violent threat at the time. Mateen entered the nightclub with an assault rifle and a pistol and began shooting. After a three-hour standoff, police crashed into the building with an armored vehicle and killed Mateen. While ISIS did not claim responsibility for the attack, the group's supporters praised Mateen's actions.

RIGHT-WING EXTREMISTS

Right-wing, anti-government extremists have also carried out terrorist attacks in the United States. These extremists believe that they are in a fight to save America and their own personal liberty. According to the Triangle Center on Terrorism and Homeland Security, many law enforcement agencies believe anti-government violent extremists are a greater threat of political violence than radicalized Islamic extremists.

They turn to violence against minorities, non-Christians, abortion providers, and government officials.

One type of right-wing extremist, called militia groups, are often organized with a military-like hierarchy. Typically, they oppose government policies and believe U.S. citizens have the right to take back the government by force if necessary. Militia extremist groups value weapons, often stockpiling weapons and ammunition, including fully automatic firearms. Some groups also make or buy improvised explosive devices (IEDs). Militia extremists often oppose gun control and see it as an unconstitutional attempt by the government to disarm citizens.

In November 2011, four members of a north Georgia militia group were arrested after a plot to bomb federal buildings, attack several cities with the poison ricin, and murder law enforcement officials was uncovered. The men scouted buildings in Atlanta to bomb and discussed a list of officials to kill in order to make the United States "right" again. In April 2012, two of the men pleaded guilty to charges of conspiring to possess explosives and firearms and were sentenced to five years in federal prison. The other two men were convicted in 2014 of conspiring to produce a toxic agent to poison government officials—they were sentenced to 10 years in prison.

SOVEREIGN CITIZENS

Another type of anti-government, right-wing extremist, called sovereign citizens, believe they are separate or sovereign, from the United States, even though they physically live within the country's borders. As sovereign citizens, these individuals believe they are not subject to federal, state, or local laws. Many of these individuals do not pay taxes, have driver's licenses, or carry Social Security cards. Additionally, they do not recognize the authority of the police or the court system.

Many sovereign citizens fight the system with paperwork. They file liens or financial claims against the personal assets of judges, police officers, or other government officials to ruin their credit. Others have been accused of crimes such as impersonating police officers or using counterfeit money and forged documents.

A few sovereign citizens have turned to violence in the name of their beliefs. These extremists have carried out violent crimes, including murder, assault, and making threats to judges, government officials, and law enforcement.

Gun control is a hotly debated issue in the United States, with people from many different backgrounds and political groups weighing in on the need for the government to regulate the gun industry.

In July 2016, Gavin Eugene Long from Kansas City, Missouri, ambushed and killed three Baton Rouge, Louisiana, police officers. A military veteran, Long died in a shootout with law enforcement. He had declared himself to be a sovereign citizen and was a member of the Washitaw Nation, a group that claimed to be a sovereign Native American nation within the United States.

The group's members believe they are above the laws of any country, state, or city. In a video recorded before the attack, Long condemned peaceful protest, saying that the only way to get back at the U.S. government was through fighting or money.

RADICAL CHRISTIAN EXTREMISTS

Radical Christian extremists believe that they are fighting a war of good vs. evil. Some of these extremists have very strong anti-abortion views. Anti-abortion activists want legalized abortion to end and the number of abortions in the United States to decrease. Most anti-abortion protesters use peaceful methods, such as marches, petitions, and rallies to spread their message.

> There are some extremists, however, who commit crimes in the name of the anti-abortion cause.

For example, in 2013, Jedediah Stout, an Iraq War veteran, was arrested in Joplin, Missouri, for attempted arson of a Planned Parenthood clinic. When questioned by investigators, Stout admitted that he was also responsible for a fire that destroyed the Islamic Society Mosque in July 2012. He called himself a conservative

Christian and told investigators that he did not like Islam and did not believe in abortion.

According to the National Abortion Federation, there were 11 murders, 26 attempted murders, 42 bombings, 185 arsons, and thousands of criminal activities directed at abortion providers and clinics in the United States between 1977 and 2015. Many extremists justify violent actions against abortion providers because they believe it to be a necessary step in their mission to protect the lives of unborn children.

In November 2015, 57-year-old Robert Lewis Dear opened fire on a Planned Parenthood clinic in Colorado Springs, Colorado. Armed with four rifles, Dear held the clinic in a standoff with police for five hours. He killed three people and wounded nine others, including five police officers. When Dear was taken into custody by law enforcement, he made statements to investigators that there would be "no more baby parts." In court, Dear claimed that he was trying to protect the babies and referred to himself as a warrior for the babies.

WHITE SUPREMACY

For decades, white supremacist groups have carried out terrorist acts in the United States. These groups, such as the Ku Klux Klan (KKK), neo-Nazis, and skinheads, see the white race as superior to other races. Simply having this belief, while offensive to many, is not illegal. However, threatening others or using violence in support of this belief is a form of terrorism and is against the law.

In November 2014, Larry Steve McQuilliams fired more than 100 rounds with a .22 caliber rifle at government buildings in Austin, Texas. He targeted a police station, a Mexican consulate, a federal courthouse, and a bank. While he was attempting to set the consulate on fire, police shot and killed McQuilliams.

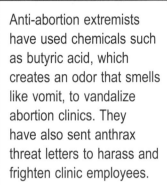

IMPACT FACT

Anti-abortion extremists have used chemicals such as butyric acid, which creates an odor that smells like vomit, to vandalize abortion clinics. They have also sent anthrax threat letters to harass and frighten clinic employees.

By attacking abortion providers and clinics, radical Christian extremists hope to limit abortion services and reduce the number of abortions in the United States.

A search of McQuilliams's van revealed homemade bombs and a map of 34 targets. Investigators also found a white supremacist book called *Vigilantes of Christendom*.

According to the FBI, there are five major subgroups within the white supremacist movement, including neo-Nazis, racist skinheads, "traditional" white supremacists, Christian Identity members, and prison gangs. Each group has its own religious or political beliefs and typically targets people of specific racial, ethnic, or religious backgrounds.

One example of this occurred in August 2012, when 40-year-old Wade Michael Page opened fire with a handgun at a Sikh temple in Oak Creek, Wisconsin. Page killed six people and wounded many others. Page was a member of the Northern Hammerskins, a violent racist skinhead group. He was also part of the white power music scene, playing in neo-Nazi rock bands End Empathy and Define Hate. After being wounded by police at the scene, Page shot and killed himself.

White supremacists such as Page have been linked to assaults, murders, threats, intimidation, and bombings. Some have also been linked to other crimes, such as drug trafficking, bank robbery, and counterfeiting.

> Frequently, white supremacists work alone or in small groups, which makes it harder for law enforcement to find them.

In October 2016, three men in Garden City, Kansas, were charged with conspiring to bomb a Somali immigrant community in Kansas. The men belonged to a group called The Crusaders, an anti-immigrant, anti-government militia.

> It's important to recognize that having beliefs isn't illegal—acting with violence in the name of those beliefs is crossing the line of the law.

IMPACT FACT

In April 2014, Frazier Glenn Cross, a former Ku Klux Klan leader, opened fire on two Jewish sites in a Kansas City, Kansas, suburb. He killed three people, including a 14-year-old boy. As police took Cross into custody, he shouted, "Heil Hitler!"

The men had stockpiled explosives and firearms to use in an attack on a building complex where many Somali immigrants lived. One of the men, Patrick Stein, told undercover agents that he hoped the attack would be a bloodbath and repeatedly referred to the immigrants as "cockroaches." What role do you think racism plays in terrorist attacks? What actions can ordinary citizens take against racism?

LONE WOLF TERRORISTS

While most terrorist acts are accomplished by groups of people, some terrorists act alone, without the help of any outside group or partners. Called lone wolf terrorists, they are motivated by a variety of ideologies, from Islamic extremism to anti-abortion and anti-government views. Because lone wolf terrorists prepare and carry out violent actions without any help or contact with an extremist group, they are often very difficult for law enforcement to identify.

Emanuel African Methodist Episcopal Church, where Dylann Roof opened fire on African American parishioners

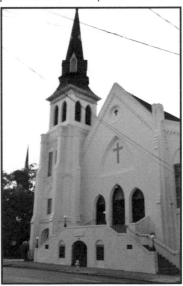

credit: Cal Sr

One of the most notorious lone wolf terrorists in the United States was Ted Kaczynski, also known as the "Unabomber." Between 1978 and 1995, Kaczynski anonymously delivered 16 mail bombs that killed three people and injured 23 others. A brilliant mathematician, Kaczynski taught at the University of California at Berkley in the late 1960s. However, he suffered from social and emotional problems and moved to the Montana woods to live as hermit in the early 1970s.

Living in almost total isolation, Kaczynski developed anti-government and anti-technology views.

In 1978, Kaczynski sent his first mail bomb. A security guard at Northwestern University was seriously injured when he opened the suspicious package. The rejection of an academic essay by two Chicago universities in 1978 might have triggered Kaczynski's letter bombing campaign. During the next 18 years, he sent 15 more bombs, targeting universities and airlines. In 1985, the first person was killed by one of his bombs. Two more would die from later bombs and many more were injured.

In 1995, Kaczynski sent a manifesto to major newspapers claiming that he would stop killing people if they published it. The document explained what Kaczynski thought to be problems in America's society. After *The Washington Post* published the document, Kaczynski's brother read it and recognized his brother's ideas and writing style. The brother contacted the FBI and told them of his suspicions, that Kaczynski was the Unabomber.

In April 1996, the FBI arrested Ted Kaczynski at his Montana cabin. Kaczynski pled guilty to more than a dozen federal charges. He was sentenced to four life sentences plus 30 years in prison.

In January 1997, a nail-laden bomb exploded outside an abortion clinic in an Atlanta suburb. After police and emergency responders arrived at the scene, a second blast exploded, injuring seven people. The next month, another bomb exploded near a crowded gay and lesbian nightclub in Atlanta, injuring several people. Investigators believe the bombings were the work of a single bomber, but they could not identify a suspect.

In January 1998, another bomb exploded at a Birmingham, Alabama, abortion clinic, killing a police officer and critically wounding a nurse. A tip led investigators to 31-year-old Eric Robert Rudolph, a self-employed carpenter. Investigators linked Rudolph to the Birmingham and Atlanta bombings and launched a manhunt.

For five years, Rudolph hid in the North Carolina Mountains and escaped capture. Law enforcement finally captured Rudolph in May 2003. After pleading guilty to four bombings and the 1998 murder of a police officer, Rudolph released an 11-page statement blaming the violence on the legalization of abortion. A judge sentenced him to life in prison.

LEFT-WING EXTREMISTS

In the 1960s, a new generation of activists emerged. These people were involved in the anti-war movement, civil rights movement, women's rights, and other political and social causes. Many people participated in peaceful protests and other non-violent methods of activism.

Some members, however, turned to violence to achieve their goals. Groups such as the Weathermen, FALN, and the Black Liberation Army carried out various violent acts on targets throughout the United States. These included attacks on police officers, bombings, and even bank robberies to fund their cause.

The group called the Weathermen (later known as the Weathermen Underground Organization) formed in June 1969 at a Students for a Democratic Society convention in Chicago. Made up of mostly white, educated, middle class young people, the group embraced violent and confrontational tactics.

TRAINWRECK SHOOTING

In July 2015, John Russell Houser opened fire at a movie theater in Lafayette, Louisiana. The theater was showing *Trainwreck*, a film starring comedian Amy Schumer. Houser killed two women and injured nine others before committing suicide. Houser reportedly promoted extreme right-wing views and was a fervent anti-feminist.

In December 1969, the Weathermen held a council in Michigan. Leaders called for bombings, armed resistance, and assassinations. By the mid-1970s, the Weathermen had bombed at least 40 targets, including the Pentagon, police stations, National Guard facilities, ROTC buildings, and the Gulf Oil headquarters in Pittsburgh, Pennsylvania. By the mid-1970s, the group's tactics changed as more members gave up armed resistance and returned to more peaceful activism. Some remaining members continued to commit acts of political violence into the 1980s.

By the early 1990s, many left-wing extremist groups had either disbanded or stopped activities. The reasons for the decline were twofold. Government forces had been generally successful at breaking up the groups. Also, by the 1990s, many groups fell apart because of a general decline in support for radical, left-wing causes.

OLYMPIC TERROR

On July 27, 1996, a nail-laden bomb exploded in Centennial Olympic Park during the 1996 Summer Olympics in Atlanta, Georgia. The explosion killed one person and injured more than one hundred others. An anonymous caller tipped off police to the bomb prior to the explosion, but it exploded before the police could stop it. Police believed the bomber intended to target law enforcement.

This statue at the Centennial Olympic Park was hit with shrapnel when a bomb exploded during the 1996 Olympics.

ECO-TERRORISM

Since the 1970s, an increasing amount of terrorist activity in the United States has been carried out by groups and individuals who support animal rights and environmental protection. Eco-terrorism is defined as acts of violence committed in support of ecological, environmental, or animal rights causes against individuals or their property.

In support of these causes, extremist groups such as the Animal Liberation Front (ALF) and the Earth Liberation Front (ELF) have carried out hundreds of attacks across the country. Most of the time, these groups have been nonviolent toward humans. Instead, they have targeted property, including buildings, monuments, laboratories, animal testing facilities, and sport-utility vehicles. ALF members oppose all forms of animal experimentation and mistreatment.

Members often work alone or in small groups to rescue animals from places of abuse.

In some cases, they commit vandalism, arson, and other attacks against people and entities that they believe to be harming animals. ALF members have claimed responsibility for hundreds of crimes, including animal releases and property destruction.

In July 2009, ALF members vandalized the home and three vehicles of Michael Selsted, a pathologist at the University of California, Irvine. They targeted Selsted to protest the animal research conducted in his lab.

Do you think it's right for humans to test medicine, cosmetics, and other products on animals? Why or why not?

ELF members target companies and individuals who profit from the destruction and exploitation of the environment. Many ELF supporters see the group's extremist actions as a way to draw public attention to their cause. ELF has claimed responsibility for hundreds of crimes in the name of environmental protection. For example, to protest development of natural lands, ELF members burned down a San Diego, California, housing complex under construction in 2003, causing property damage of around $50 million.

To protest the environmental damage caused by sport-utility vehicles (SUVs) and other cars, ELF members have also targeted auto dealerships. Members have set fire to dealerships and burned and vandalized cars and SUVs. In 2009, members of ELF toppled two radio towers near Seattle because of health and environmental concerns. They left a sign with the letters "ELF" near the towers.

Eco-Arson

ELF has been linked to several other crimes of arson, including the 2008 burning of four luxury homes in the suburbs of Seattle, Washington, and the 2001 arson that destroyed the University of Washington's Center for Urban Horticulture. How do terrorists justify violence in the name of protecting the environment?

RADICALIZATION

What causes a person to become a terrorist? Through a process of radicalization, individuals can gradually adopt extremist views. Radicalization is not unique to any religion, ethnic group, nationality, or gender. Anyone can be a potential sympathizer with a terrorist group if conditions are right. Not everyone who adopts radical views will take the next step and carry out a violent attack. But some will.

There is no single model of how a person radicalizes. Those who do tend to come from very different backgrounds, are attracted to an extreme ideology for different reasons, and take different paths to radicalization. Prison, the Internet, social media, and personal connections with family and friends who are already radicalized are the most common ways a person becomes exposed to extremist ideologies.

They can be exposed to these ideas by reading propaganda on the Internet or spending time with a friend who is already radicalized. They may interact with strangers on social media who seem to have profound and exciting ideas.

The most common theme is simply being exposed to the ideology. That is why terror groups such as ISIS spread their propaganda in many places and in many forms, in order to reach as many people as possible. Some groups even use recruiters who actively seek out people who may be likely to radicalize.

Aqsa Mahmood is a young woman from a wealthy neighborhood in Scotland. As a child and young teen, Mahmood did not appear to have any extremist beliefs, according to her parents. Like many Western and American teens, she read Harry Potter books and enjoyed going to the movies with her sisters. When civil war broke out in Syria, Mahmood became concerned about the violence. She began praying and reading the Qur'an.

Syria is not only a place of civil war, it is also the location of some of the earliest human civilizations. This village, called Serjilla, thrived around 473.

credit: James Gordon

Soon, she gave up music and childhood fiction. She spent increasing amounts of time in her bedroom, away from parents and friends, watching Muslim sermons and interacting in radical Muslim chat forums with people she met online. In 2013, Mahmood dropped out of Glasgow University at the age of 19 to marry an ISIS fighter in Syria. She is now one of the terror group's top recruiters, often talking about the virtues of being a jihadist bride on social media.

Other examples of radicalization can be found across the United States. On December 2, 2015, workers at the San Bernardino County, California, health department gathered for a training session. One of the department's employees, Syed Rizwan Farook, left the session and returned with his wife, Tashfeen Malik. Together, the couple began shooting at the employees, firing more than 100 rounds before escaping. Four hours later, police killed them in a gun battle on a residential street. The terrorist attack killed 14 people and wounded 22 others. Prior to the attack, Malik was reported to have sent a pledge of allegiance on Facebook to Islamic State leader Abu Bakr al-Baghdadi.

The couple was not known to law enforcement as a potential threat. Born in Chicago to Pakistani immigrant parents, Farook worked as an environmental health specialist for San Bernardino County. He met his wife, Malik, through an online dating service. She came to the United States on a fiancée visa and became a legal permanent resident. The couple lived in a two-story townhouse with their infant daughter in a middle-class neighborhood.

Coworkers and neighbors described Farook as a quiet and deeply religious man who displayed no warning signs of violence.

FBI investigators said that the couple were homegrown violent extremists inspired to carry out their terror attack by foreign terrorist groups. They were not directed by a foreign group and were not part of any terrorist organization. Instead, investigators believe that Farook and Malik had become radicalized over a period of several years through material on the Internet.

A trip to Saudi Arabia a few years before the attack might have contributed to their radicalization. When law enforcement searched their home, they found a large stockpile of weapons, ammunition, and bomb-making equipment.

Homegrown terrorists have killed American citizens and caused millions of dollars of property damage across the United States. Domestic terror groups support a wide variety of extremist ideologies and movements. Their targets vary by group and can include civilians, commercial entities, government officials and sites, and military targets. These terrorists use a variety of weapons and tactics, from bombs and guns to arson and mass shootings. While many Americans fear foreign terror groups, some of the most deadly attacks on American soil have been carried out by people already here.

VOCAB LAB

Write down what you think each word means. What root words can you find to help you? What does the context of the word tell you?

eco-terrorist, left wing, lone wolf, manifesto, militia group, neo-Nazi, race war, radicalization, right wing, skinhead, sovereign citizen, vandalism, and **white supremacy**.

Compare your definitions with those of your friends or classmates. Did you all come up with the same meanings? Turn to the text and glossary if you need help.

KEY QUESTIONS

- **Are there connections between the policies of the United States government and the radicalization of its citizens? Why might ordinary citizens seek solutions in radical violence?**

- **Why do many people in the United States fear foreign terrorists more than American terrorists?**

- **Can you think of events in American history that are now thought of as necessary rebellions that were considered acts of terrorism at the time?**

THE PROCESS OF RADICALIZATION

The process of radicalization is different for every individual. While the path each person takes toward adopting extremist views is different, are there some similarities? By studying the radicalization of several different individuals, you can look for common themes in their stories.

- **The stories of radicalization for several people can be found online.** You can read and listen them here.

  Alex, a 23-year-old Sunday school teacher and babysitter

  Dzhokhar Tsarnaev, one of the Boston Marathon bombers

  Mohammed Hamzah Khan, a Chicago teenager

- **After reading each of their stories, consider what factors made each person susceptible to becoming radicalized.**

  - What similarities did you find in their paths to radicalization?

  - What differences?

  - What outcomes did each individual have?

  - What made their outcomes different?

To investigate more, after learning about the process of radicalization, what safeguards would you suggest to prevent American teens from adopting extreme, radical views? Prepare a presentation of your ideas.

Chapter 5 ▶
The Fight Against Terrorism

What are some of the ways people around the world can work to combat terrorism?

There are many different techniques countries can use to disrupt plans for terrorism, including negotiation, force, and surveillance.

When terrorists attack, countries face a dilemma. How should they respond? Some governments choose to negotiate with terror groups, while others choose a more forceful response. Many countries have taken steps to prevent terrorism before it occurs by enhancing security procedures or sending out intelligence agents to gather information.

Regardless of the tactics chosen, the ultimate goal is the same—to save lives by preventing or reducing the number of terror attacks.

NEGOTIATION

In some cases, negotiation can be a successful strategy for dealing with and preventing future terror acts. For example, although Israel is generally tough on terrorism, it has occasionally negotiated with terrorists.

In 1985, Hezbollah terrorists hijacked TWA Flight 847 leaving Athens, Greece, and forced it to fly to Beirut, Lebanon. They held the passengers hostage and demanded that Israel release more than 700 Hezbollah prisoners. The terrorists killed one passenger, U.S. Navy diver Robert Stethem, and tossed his body onto the airport tarmac.

With several Americans among the hostages, the U.S. government pressured the Israeli government to negotiate for their release through a series of intermediaries. Eventually, the terrorists and Israel were able to agree to the release of the rest of the hostages in exchange for the release of the Hezbollah prisoners.

Negotiation can be successful in certain situations because it focuses on the underlying reasons people turn to terrorism. In particular, governments have had success negotiating with terror groups that harbor nationalist motives. These groups often have a clearly defined goal, such as the ability to govern themselves. They also have support from a large number of people both in their own country and in other governments and groups around the world.

For example, in Northern Ireland, negotiations between the Provisional Irish Republican Army and the British government eventually led to the Good Friday Agreement in 1998. This was a landmark agreement between most of the main political parties in Northern Ireland and the British and Irish governments that renounced violence. It established a new Northern Ireland legislative assembly, increased cross-border ties, and freed prisoners. The agreement also called for the disarming of all paramilitary groups.

IMPACT FACT

Although several splinter groups tried to sabotage the peace process, the Good Friday Agreement between the IRA and the British government was the start of a long-term reduction in terrorist violence. In July 2005, the IRA announced an end to armed struggle and ordered its members to stop violent actions.

Negotiation as a strategy to deal with terrorists can be tricky. If the negotiations aren't handled properly, governments that negotiate with terrorists can appear weak. Other terror groups may think that they can blackmail the government with future terror acts to achieve their goals. Citizens may resent the government for "giving in" to terrorists. And the terrorists themselves may have a hard time coming together to negotiate with a government that they view as an enemy.

FORCE

In some cases, countries have chosen military options to respond to terrorism. Some military strikes focus on targets linked to terrorists. These strikes intend to destroy or significantly disrupt a terrorist group's infrastructure and injure or kill its members. Punitive strikes aim to punish terrorist targets, often in response to a terror attack. Often, these types of strikes are planned to destroy specific facilities or group members or leaders.

For example, after the attacks of September 11, 2001, the United States declared itself at war against global terrorism. Joined by several allies, the United States launched Operation Enduring Freedom. The military campaign began with the October 2001 invasion of Afghanistan. Military personnel set out to destroy Al-Qaeda's safe havens in Afghanistan, collect intelligence against the terror network, disrupt Al-Qaeda's operations, and capture and kill as many Al-Qaeda members as possible.

In contrast to a large military strike, sometimes the use of force can be much smaller in scope and have a very narrow goal. Covert operations are secret missions such as assassinations, sabotage of facilities or supplies, and kidnappings. Special operations forces that are trained in covert operations typically carry out these types of missions.

On May 2, 2011, U.S. Navy special forces carried out a covert operation that killed Al-Qaeda leader Osama bin Laden in Abbottabad, Pakistan. After years of work, U.S. intelligence officers tracked bin Laden to a compound in Abbottabad. Military leaders deployed the special forces unit known as SEAL Team Six to strike. Once ready, the SEALs launched a night-time helicopter-borne attack on May 2. When they raided the compound, they found bin Laden on an upper floor of the compound's main building and shot him dead. Four other bin Laden associates were also killed during the assault.

INTELLIGENCE

Many nations, including the United States, deploy intelligence agents to collect information about terrorist activities and terror group members. While intelligence information alone cannot stop a terror attack, it is an important first step in identifying and preventing one.

Intelligence agencies collect information in many different ways. They use local police to gather information about criminal activity that might have ties to terror suspects. They monitor terror suspects, tracking their movements in and out of countries. They also use surveillance at certain sites to identify suspicious activity. Some agents monitor social media sites and other online activity, searching for information about terrorist threats.

Intelligence agencies analyze all of the information they receive about terror groups. They build databases that can be used to predict terrorist behavior. Expert intelligence analysts create profiles of terrorist organizations and track the movements of individual terrorists. With this analysis, intelligence agents hope to be able to anticipate terrorist behavior and predict terror attacks before they occur, so that agencies can defend against them.

IMPACT FACT

Before the assault on Osama bin Laden, approximately two dozen SEAL commandos practiced every step of the planned strike.

In the United States, the FBI performs domestic intelligence collection, while the Central Intelligence Agency (CIA) handles international intelligence. In some cases, intelligence agents go undercover to infiltrate terror groups. Undercover, they can disrupt planned operations, spread disinformation, identify group members, and do other things to prevent terror attacks.

STOPPING A TERROR ATTACK

On February 17, 2012, Amine Mohamed El-Khalifi pulled his car into a parking garage in Washington, DC. The 29-year-old northern Virginia resident came to visit the United States Capitol building. He brought a vest covered with explosives and an assault rifle. He planned to blow himself up at the entrance to the Capitol building, killing as many people as he could. If anyone got in his way, he would shoot them with the assault rifle.

For months, El-Khalifi had planned the details of the attack, which he would carry out in the name of jihad, a holy war waged on behalf of Islam. A Moroccan citizen, El-Khalifi had come to the United States more than 10 years earlier. At first, El-Khalifi had embraced Western culture. But in 2010, he began posting radical jihadist messages on the Internet. He showed an interest in joining the mujahedeen, the Muslim guerilla warriors fighting a holy war in the Middle East, in Afghanistan. FBI agents who investigated El-Khalifi believed that he became radicalized online.

In January 2011, El-Khalifi met with people who encouraged jihad. By the end of 2011, El-Khalifi was actively looking to join an armed extremist group. He also talked about bombing attacks on specific targets, such as a local synagogue and a restaurant popular with American military officials.

El-Khalifi met a man named Yusuf in 2011. He believed Yusuf was an Al-Qaeda operative. El-Khalifi talked with Yusuf about planning an attack in the United States. What El-Khalifi didn't know, however, was that Yusuf was actually an undercover FBI agent. The FBI's Washington Field Office Joint Terrorism Task Force (JTTF) had identified El-Khalifi as a threat and was monitoring his every move.

During meetings with the undercover agent, El-Khalifi tested weapons and explosives. In January 2012, he decided to attack the Capitol on a suicide mission, visiting the building several times to scout out the site. On the day of the planned attack, El-Khalifi emerged from his car, put on the suicide vest, and prepared to die. Instead, FBI agents moved in and arrested him as he walked to the Capitol.

Unknown to El-Khalifi, FBI technicians had made the explosives in his vest and his rifle inoperable. El-Khalifi pled guilty to the attempted use of a weapon of mass destruction. He was sentenced to 30 years in prison.[1]

This is one example of a case in which intelligence gathering and the use of undercover agents successfully prevented a terrorist attack.

Sometimes terror attacks are stopped by citizens. Here, Secretary of Defense Ash Carter, Deputy Secretary of Defense Robert O. Work, and 10th Vice Chairman of the Joint Chiefs of Staff Gen. Paul J. Selva honor Anthony Sadler (second from left) for halting an attack on a train in France in 2015.

STING OPERATIONS

The FBI frequently uses sting operations to uncover terror plots. In a sting operation, an undercover agent will often pose as a potential terrorist or sympathizer and discuss terror plots and targets with terror suspects. Agents identify suspects via online activity that promotes violence or through tips from confidential informants. After a suspect receives weapons or fake explosives, agents arrest them. Many people believe that sting operations are an important tool for preventing terrorism. Others challenge these operations and argue that suspects are entrapped and groomed by investigators.

ENHANCED SECURITY PROCEDURES

Many countries have also enhanced security procedures to combat terrorism. Security barriers, checkpoints, and surveillance are common security measures used to deter terrorism. By making it harder to carry out an attack, enhanced security helps prevent a terrorist from selecting a certain site as a target. After the 1993 World Trade Center and 1995 Oklahoma City bombings, both of which were carried out by car and truck bombs, all traffic was blocked on Pennsylvania Avenue in front of the White House in order to reduce any threat.

Security checkpoints at land borders, ports, and airports have also become stricter in recent years. At many airports, several changes have been made since 9/11 to improve security. Passengers and their luggage are carefully screened before they can board a plane. Cockpit doors have been strengthened to prevent terrorists from taking over planes.

Some flights even have sky marshals dressed as regular passengers, who carry weapons and can deal with potential terrorist situations in-flight.

In some cases, countries have even built walls and fences to deter terror attacks. Israel has built a network of fences and surveillance posts along its border with Jordan to prevent Palestinian fighters from easily entering Israel. It also constructed another fence along its border with the West Bank after bombings and other attacks killed hundreds of Israelis.

IMPACT FACT

In northwest Africa, Morocco built a sand and earthen wall in the 1980s to protect against a Saharan nationalist group called the Polisario. The wall stretched for more than 1,200 miles.

ECONOMIC SANCTIONS

Countries have used economic sanctions as a non-military way to discourage terrorism. Economic sanctions are often meant to punish or disrupt state sponsors of terrorism. Often, this type of sanction takes the form of trade restrictions and controls. By imposing economic sanctions, governments hope to put pressure on nations to end their support for terrorism and terror groups. Sanctions also serve as a public condemnation of the sanctioned country's behavior.

Economic sanctions are a long-term strategy. It can take months, even years, for a sanctioned country to feel the effects of trade restrictions. And in order for economic sanctions to be successful, the international community must remain united and control any trade leaks. In addition, the members of the sanctioned government, not just the citizens, must be affected by the sanctions.

In 1982, the United States banned imports of oil from Libya and restricted U.S. exports to the country. The United States placed these sanctions in response to the Libyan government's sponsorship of international terrorism. During the next few years, the United States increased its pressure on Libya by expanding its economic sanctions. By 1986, the United States totally banned all direct import and export trade, commercial contracts, and travel activities. In addition, it froze any Libyan government assets in the United States.

After the 1988 bombing of Pan Am Flight 103 over Lockerbie, Scotland, when Libya refused to extradite two men suspected of planning the bombing, the United Nations (UN) Security Council also imposed economic sanctions. Eventually, the United States and international sanctions pressured Libya to renounce terrorism.

ANTI-TERRORISM AND EFFECTIVE DEATH PENALTY ACT

In 1995, the United States passed the Anti-Terrorism and Effective Death Penalty Act, the country's first comprehensive counterterrorism legislation. The act's goal is to regulate activity that could be used to carry out a terrorist attack, provide resources for counterterrorist programs, and punish terrorism. The act includes a federal death penalty when acts of terrorism result in deaths.

In 2002, Libya offered to pay $10 million in compensation for each victim of the Lockerbie bombing in exchange for the lifting of economic sanctions. After Libya dismantled its WMD program and allowed international inspectors into the country, most UN and U.S. sanctions were lifted.

UNITED NATIONS

Because terrorism is global, countries often need to work together to successfully fight terrorism. The UN has an important role in working toward this goal. Established in 1945 after World War II, the UN is an organization of countries whose main goal is to promote world peace.

Prior to 2001, the UN passed several anti-terrorism resolutions. Each one focused on a different type of terror activity, such as bombings and hijackings. Several countries signed the resolutions and agreed to introduce security measures to prevent future attacks. Some resolutions created greater restrictions on terrorist funds, weapons, and other assets. However, not all countries signed these resolutions.

> Some countries believe that people have a right to use force in the struggle against foreign oppression.

After the September 11, 2001, terrorist attacks in the United States, representatives from countries around the world gathered at the UN's New York City headquarters, which is just a mile from the terrorist attack site. On September 28, 2001, they unanimously passed an international response to the attack.

WE RESOLVE

You can read Security Council Resolution 1373 at this site. Do you think this resolution would have read differently if it had been written a year after 9/11? Why? What was symbolic about hosting the meeting in New York City, so close to the site of the World Trade Center? How did this affect the people who attended, and how did it affect the people who were watching all around the world?

🔍 UNSCR 1373 text

Security Council Resolution 1373 (UNSCR 1373) called for nations to freeze terrorist financing, pass anti-terrorism laws, prevent suspected terrorists from traveling across country borders, require that asylum seekers be screened for possible terrorist connections, and share information about groups planning terrorist attacks.

The resolution also established the UN's Counter-Terrorism Committee (CTC). The CTC works to assist UN member countries to prevent terrorism in their countries and across borders. The UN later established the Counter-Terrorism Committee Executive Directorate (CTED), which works to strengthen and coordinate the implementation of UN Security Council resolutions. It also conducts country assessments and identifies areas for improvement.

The UN Security Council has issued several other resolutions related to terrorism since UNSCR 1373, often in response to a specific crisis. In 2006, the UN General Assembly unanimously passed the UN Global Counterterrorism Strategy, and reaffirmed it in 2008 and 2010. The strategy details UN counterterrorism activities in a single document. It is based on four pillars: addressing the conditions that allow the spread of terrorism, preventing and fighting terrorism, building country and UN counterterrorism efforts, and ensuring respect for the protection of human rights in counterterrorism efforts.[2]

Today, the UN's counterterrorism efforts include 16 conventions and protocols, several Security Council resolutions, and the UN Global Counter-Terrorism Strategy. Yet, because member states still do not agree on a definition of terrorism, there has been little progress on a comprehensive world treaty against terrorism. Why does a lack of a global definition of terrorism stand in the way of fighting it?

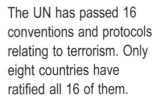

IMPACT FACT

The UN has passed 16 conventions and protocols relating to terrorism. Only eight countries have ratified all 16 of them.

On occasion, the UN has imposed sanctions on nations that sponsor terrorism. The UN may direct member nations to stop trading with the sanctioned country or to sever diplomatic relations and suspend communications. The UN imposed sanctions on Libya after the bombings of Pan Am Flight 103 in 1988 and UTA Flight 772 in 1989, and on Sudan in 1995 after the attempted assassination of Egypt's Hosni Mubarak by terrorists based in Sudan. Sanctions against the Taliban government in Afghanistan included a limited air embargo and assets freeze in 1999 because it was giving shelter to Al-Qaeda. Eventually, the sanctions included a travel ban and arms embargo.

It has been difficult to measure the effectiveness of the UN's efforts against terrorism. However, the UN does coordinate the counterterrorism policies of multiple countries and give member nations support to combat terrorism in their own countries or in partnership with other nations.

HOMELAND SECURITY IN THE UNITED STATES

Within the United States, several agencies and law enforcement groups work to prevent terrorism. After the September 11, 2001, attacks on the United States, Congress passed the Department of Homeland Security Act of 2002, which was signed into law by President George W. Bush in November 2002. The act created the Department of Homeland Security (DHS).

The act completely reorganized the country's counterterrorism efforts and consolidated 22 federal agencies and bureaus under the newly created department. These included the U.S Coast Guard, Federal Emergency Management Agency, U.S. Immigration and Customs Enforcement, U.S. Customs and Border Protection, and more.

The DHS is the third-largest department in the U.S. government. DHS's mission is to protect the United States from threats, including terrorism. It secures the country's borders and makes sure that people entering, living, and working in the United States are legally allowed in the country. DHS also protects the country's computer systems from cyberattacks.

FBI: PROTECTING AMERICANS

Within the United States, the FBI is the lead agency in terrorism cases. FBI agents work to identify and prevent terrorism acts before they occur. When an act of terror occurs, the FBI takes the lead on the immediate response to the crisis. In the days and weeks after the incident, the FBI heads the investigation.

To prevent terrorism in the United States, the FBI works closely with many federal, state, and local agencies to disrupt and investigate acts of terrorism. Agencies such as the Bureau of Alcohol, Tobacco, Firearms and Explosives and the Internal Revenue Service play roles in preventing terrorism.

> Specialists and agents from these agencies work with state and local law enforcement to uncover and disrupt terror plots.

Together, these partners gather, archive, and analyze massive amounts of information on American citizens and other people living in the United States. They also investigate tips reported by law enforcement officers and ordinary citizens about people acting suspiciously in the community.

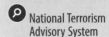

CATEGORIES OF THREAT

In 2011, the DHS introduced a new system to warn Americans about threats. Threats are put into either "elevated" or "imminent" categories. The DHS makes public announcements when it has new information about threats. You can see the system at the following link.

🔍 National Terrorism Advisory System

U.S. INTELLIGENCE AGENCIES

In addition to the FBI, several intelligence agencies work to prevent terrorism in the United States.

- The National Security Agency uses state-of-the-art computer and satellite technology to collect communications and other signal intelligence. It also uses its technological expertise for code-making and code-breaking activities.

- The CIA is a federal agency that collects intelligence outside U.S. borders. It uses human intelligence agents and technology to do so. It is against the law for the CIA to collect intelligence about U.S. citizens or U.S. organizations.

- The Defense Intelligence Agency is the central intelligence bureau for the U.S. military. It coordinates intelligence collection and analysis among all branches of the military.

The Memorial Wall at the CIA headquarters. Each star stands for a fallen agent.

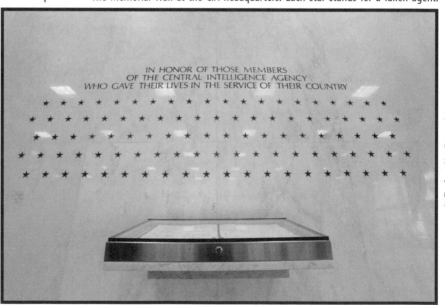

credit: The Central Intelligence Agency

USA PATRIOT ACT

After the 9/11 attacks on the United States, U.S. Attorney General John Ashcroft presented to Congress a list of recommended changes to the law. The changes were designed to allow the country to combat terrorism more effectively. The U.S. Congress quickly passed these changes, which it named the USA Patriot Act.

The USA Patriot Act reduces restrictions on law enforcement's ability to investigate possible terrorist plots. It eases restrictions on searching telephone, email, medical, financial, and other records. It can also require banks to identify sources of money deposited in some private accounts or order foreign banks to report suspicious transactions. It permits the use of roving wiretaps, which allow surveillance of any person's telephone conversations on any phone, anywhere in the country. It also allows immigrants to be detained without charge for up to one week on suspicion of supporting terrorism, and the deportation of immigrants who raise money for terrorist organizations.

The USA Patriot Act expands the definition of terrorism to include domestic terrorism.

The USA Patriot Act defines domestic terrorism as activities within the United States that involve illegal acts dangerous to human life, if the act appears to be intended to intimidate or coerce a civilian population, influence government policy through intimidation or coercion, or affect a government's actions through mass destruction, assassination, or kidnapping. The USA Patriot Act was renewed in March 2006.

PERCEPTIONS

In a December 2015 Pew Research Center survey, 56 percent of Americans believed that the government's anti-terror policies had not done enough to protect the country, while 28 percent expressed concern that the policies had gone too far in restricting the average person's civil liberties.

The full name of the USA Patriot Act is Uniting and Strengthening America by Providing Appropriate Tools Required to Intercept and Obstruct Terrorism

SURVEILLANCE VS. PRIVACY AND HUMAN RIGHTS

Intelligence officials say that government surveillance efforts used since the 9/11 attacks have helped prevent many terrorist events in the United States. At the same time, surveillance conducted in the name of preventing terrorism can easily cross the line and violate the privacy and constitutional rights of American citizens.

In 2014, the American Civil Liberties Union (ACLU) and other civil rights groups filed a lawsuit challenging the government's Suspicious Activity Reporting (SAR) program. Implemented after 9/11, SAR encourages local police to create suspicious activity reports, based on federal guidance, when they encounter people whose behavior causes concern that they might be involved in a terror plot. The reports are received, stored, and analyzed at dozens of state and federal information centers nationwide.

According to the ACLU, the program encourages racial and religious profiling, wrongly targets activities protected by the First Amendment, and violates federal law. In 2017, a federal judge ruled against the case, stating that the standard used by the program to identify possible terror activity was legally adopted and not arbitrary.

Although there are concerns about privacy, the majority of American adults believe in a security-first approach, even if it infringes on the privacy rights of citizens.

JOINT TERRORISM TASK FORCE

Under the USA Patriot Act, joint terrorism task forces (JTTFs) were established. There are more than 100 JTTFs across the country. Each is a highly trained, locally based team of police officers, federal agents, investigators, analysts, linguists, SWAT experts, and other specialists. Members come from dozens of U.S. law enforcement and intelligence agencies. Each JTTF investigates acts of terrorism, develops informants, and gathers intelligence to prevent terrorist plots. The JTTFs also share FBI intelligence with outside agencies and law enforcement.

Sometimes, governments have found it difficult to balance the need to prevent terrorism with the ongoing protection of human rights. After 9/11, some critics argued that the United States and its allies used counterterrorism tactics that weakened international human rights laws.

These tactics included enhanced interrogation and torture of terrorism suspects, the transfer of detainees without legal process to the custody of a foreign government for detention and interrogation, the suspension of ordinary due process, and indefinite detention at the U.S. facility at Guantanamo Bay, Cuba. However, some people believe that the use of enhanced interrogation tactics or indefinite detention of potentially dangerous people is justified because it may prevent the next terror attack.

Terrorism threats are complex and diverse. The next violent attack could come from any number of groups, ideologies, and individuals. Because of law enforcement and citizen efforts, many terror plots have been prevented before anyone was hurt or any property was damaged. As long as the threat of terrorism exists, governments and law enforcement officials around the world will continue to work to protect people from the next terror attack.

KEY QUESTIONS

- **What are the pros and cons of using force to defeat terrorism? What about the pros and cons of negotiation? Economic sanctions? Is one better than the other?**

- **What can countries learn about different terrorists through social media sites?**

- **Is it important for the public to be a part of the debate about new legislation meant to protect against terrorism, such as the USA Patriot Act? Why or why not?**

VOCAB LAB

Write down what you think each word means. What root words can you find to help you? What does the context of the word tell you?

covert operation, **deportation**, **economic sanctions**, **human rights**, **infiltrate**, **negotiation**, **profiling**, **punitive strike**, **sabotage**, and **surveillance**.

Compare your definitions with those of your friends or classmates. Did you all come up with the same meanings? Turn to the text and glossary if you need help.

PRIVACY AND NATIONAL SECURITY

Many organizations can give you background information on the issue of privacy rights and national security needs. Try these.

🔍 CNBC privacy

🔍 Pew Research Center privacy

🔍 Newsweek privacy

To investigate more, write a persuasive essay taking the other side of the debate. Use your essay to persuade the reader to agree with your position.

PRIVACY VS. NATIONAL SECURITY

In 2016, the FBI asked Apple to help unlock the iPhone belonging to Syed Rizwan Farook, the man responsible for the 2015 San Bernardino, California, terrorist attack. Apple refused, saying that doing so would violate data privacy rights. While the case was being argued in court, the FBI used the expertise of a third party to unlock the phone for its investigation. This case highlights the struggle to balance privacy rights and national security needs.

- **Read some background information about privacy rights vs. national security needs.** As you research the issue, think about the following questions.

  - Is it possible to find a balance between protecting the country and individual privacy? Has the government found the right balance?

  - Do you think the government should be more concerned with national security or privacy rights in its surveillance programs?

  - What kind of information do you think the government should have access to in order to prevent terror attacks?

- **Prepare for a debate.** Use the following prompt: Should American citizens be willing to give up some privacy in exchange for increased security against terrorism?

- **As you prepare, note what strong points you will make in your argument.** Then, try to think of what the opposing side might say against you and prepare responses.

PREVENTING TERROR ATTACKS

While successful terror attacks make headlines around the world, there are dozens of plots that have been thwarted by counterterrorism efforts. You can read about some of these plots here.

  Heritage Foundation counterterrorism

* **Select three or four thwarted terror plots to research.** Find and read newspaper or magazine articles about the foiled attacks.

* **Create a chart to categorize the plots.**

  * What types of attacks were planned?

  * What methods did terrorists use?

  * Who was involved?

  * What targets did they choose?

  * What was the objective?

  * How was the plot stopped?

  * What counterterrorism methods were used?

  * What was the outcome?

* **Does the number of thwarted terror plots make you feel more or less secure?** Explain.

> **To investigate more,** compare what you have learned about the thwarted terror plots to a successful terror attack (for example, San Bernardino, Orlando, or Paris). Why do you think one attack was successful, while others were not?

AIRPORT SECURITY AND CIVIL RIGHTS

After 9/11, U.S. officials enhanced security at all airports. These security measures included screenings of all passengers and their luggage, plus restrictions on items allowed in carry-on bags. In addition, certain passengers can be selected for full-body scans, body searches, and questioning.

While some enhanced security procedures apply to all passengers, others, such as body searches and questioning, are applied only to a select group. How does airport security choose who to search or question? Do the enhanced procedures violate the passengers' civil rights?

- **Consider the following methods airport security could use to apply these enhanced security procedures to passengers:**

  - Search everyone

  - Search random people

  - Use profiling to decide who is searched

  - Search no one

- **What are the pros and cons of each method?**

  - How does each method impact passenger rights and security?

  - Are any civil rights being violated in any of these scenarios?

  - What actions do you think security officials should take? Why?

> **To investigate more,** conduct a poll of classmates, family, and friends about their opinions on airport security procedures and national security. Design poll questions and track responses. Present your results in a chart or graph. Can you find any patterns?

Chapter 6 ▶
The Future of Terrorism

How does technology contribute to terrorism and counterterrorism?

By using available technology to monitor and disrupt terrorist strategies while improving relationships within communities, people can feel safer and more secure both at home and while traveling in different countries.

For thousands of years, terrorism has affected people of all nationalities and ethnic and religious backgrounds. Throughout the years, terrorism has adapted its methods and tactics to take advantage of changing technologies and societies. And despite an increased focus on identifying and preventing terror threats since 9/11, terrorism remains a serious concern in the United States and around the world.

Although the death of Osama bin Laden in May 2011 was a victory in the global war against terrorism, the fight is not over. Recent attacks by terror groups and individuals show that terrorism still poses a significant threat worldwide. In 2015, terrorist attacks occurred in 92 different countries.[1]

Modern terror groups have found it easier to cross country borders, recruit members worldwide, and carry out attacks in different countries. Terrorists have shown an increasing ability to adapt to counterterrorism measures, develop new ways to attack, and improve existing tactics and methods.

COMBATTING ISIS

According to the U.S. State Department, the Islamic State of Iraq and the Levant, also known as ISIL, has become the world's greatest terror threat. Also known as ISIS and Islamic State, the militant group follows a fundamentalist doctrine of Sunni Islam. In 2014, ISIS fighters captured territories in western Iraq and eastern Syria, with the goal of establishing a state.

Originally part of Osama bin Laden's Al-Qaeda organization, ISIS split to form its own group. After capturing the cities of Mosul and Tikrit in Iraq in June 2014, ISIS proclaimed itself a caliphate, in which it claimed exclusive political and theological authority over the world's Muslim population.

Highly publicized military successes have attracted thousands of foreign recruits to the group, including many Western nationals. Intelligence agencies around the world have expressed concern that citizens from their countries who have joined the fighting in Iraq and Syria will become radicalized and then return to their home countries to carry out attacks.

The United States, the UN, and many individuals have designated ISIS as a terrorist organization. The UN has also charged ISIS with human rights abuses and war crimes.

In the end of 2015, ISIS fighters carried out a series of attacks in France, Lebanon, and Turkey. These attacks demonstrated the group's ability to carry out deadly terror plots outside of Iraq and Syria. The attacks also exposed weaknesses in international border security systems and procedures that can be exploited by terror groups.

THE ROLE OF ISIS

This short video provides a clear and concise overview of ISIS and its role in the region.

 Wall Street Journal ISIS explained

IMPACT FACT

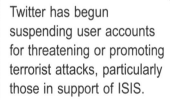

Twitter has begun suspending user accounts for threatening or promoting terrorist attacks, particularly those in support of ISIS.

ISIS finances its operations through extortion, taxes on local populations, oil smuggling, kidnapping for ransom, looting, foreign donations, and human trafficking.

An Iraqi soldier prepares for chemical warfare when fighting ISIS.

Along with its planned actions, ISIS has been able to inspire terror attacks by non-affiliated people and small groups. These self-radicalized people live in countries around the world and often have never been to Iraq or Syria. Instead, the Internet and social media has allowed them to access ISIS's propaganda and use it to inspire their own violent acts.

IMPACT FACT

Between 1990 and 2014 in the United States, there were 39 deadly terror attacks committed by extremists associated with Al-Qaeda. During that same period, there were 178 deadly attacks by far-right extremists.[2]

THE RISE OF HOMEGROWN VIOLENT EXTREMISTS

Homegrown violent extremists are another growing terror threat. In recent years, the number of American citizens or permanent residents who were radicalized and recruited to carry out Islamic terrorist activities has increased significantly. Between 2007 and 2013, 60 Islamist-inspired terror plots were uncovered in the United States. Out of those, 49 could be considered homegrown terror plots, planned by American citizens, legal permanent residents, or visitors radicalized mostly in the United States.

In one plot, brothers Raees Alam Qazi and Sheheryar Alam Qazi were arrested and charged with conspiring to detonate a weapon of mass destruction and providing material support to terrorists in November 2012. Born in Pakistan, the brothers were naturalized U.S. citizens and lived in Oakland Park, Florida. To avenge deaths caused by military drone strikes in Afghanistan, the brothers planned to carry out a suicide attack or remote control bombing at potential targets in New York City, including Times Square, Wall Street, and Broadway theaters. Fortunately, law enforcement thwarted the attack and arrested the men before they could carry out their deadly plan.

DECENTRALIZED OPERATIONS

After the 9/11 attacks in New York, counterterrorism officials focused on finding and stopping centralized terror networks. These large groups were well-financed and organized. Security officials feared these centralized terrorist groups had the ability to carry out another large-scale, detailed attack against a target.

In recent years, terrorist activity has become increasingly more decentralized. People with little or no connection to known terrorist groups have attempted to carry out attacks. No longer do they need to train with an extremist group in the Middle East—now, smaller groups can plan and prepare attacks thousands of miles away, using information they find on the Internet. They can communicate that way, too.

Although these individual attacks have been smaller in scale than the 9/11 attacks, they still have the potential to be deadly. Terrorist experts believe that this trend is occurring because the larger terror networks are not as well organized as they were in the past. Also, many smaller groups and people want to make a name for themselves. There can be fame in terrorism. Why might this be attractive for some people?

RIGHT-WING EXTREMISTS

According to the Southern Poverty Law Center, there were 437 incidents of intimidation between the November 8 election and November 14, 2016. These incidents targeted African Americans and other people of color, Muslims, immigrants, the lesbian/bisexual/gay/transgender (LBGT) community, and women. Johnathan Greenblatt, the national director of the Anti-Defamation League, reported that his group also saw a spike in reports of harassment, vandalism, and physical violence. These events of right-wing extremism occurred after one of the most controversial elections in the history of the United States. Why do you think this happened?

MORE LONE WOLF ATTACKS

As terror operations become more decentralized, the number of lone wolf attacks are increasing. As you learned earlier in the book, sometimes, an individual is driven by their beliefs to commit terrorist acts alone, without a larger group's knowledge or support. These people, called lone wolf terrorists, can plan attacks that are just as deadly as those carried out by a larger, organized group. A single bomb can bring down an airplane, killing hundreds of innocent victims. A single gunman can kill and wound dozens of people.

Often, it is nearly impossible for law enforcement to identify a lone wolf attacker, unless the person reaches out to others for guidance. In recent years, there has been an increase in terror attacks in the United States and abroad being committed by lone wolf attackers, a trend that experts predict will continue into the future.

Law enforcement will need to adjust its strategies and tactics to better track and prevent lone wolf terrorism.

Today's lone wolfs have access to a variety of deadly weapons, including machine guns, bombs, and chemical and biological weapons.

HIGH-TECH TERRORISM

New technologies such as the Internet and social media have made it easier for terrorists to communicate from anywhere in the world and to spread their message globally. Extremists are already using the Internet to spread propaganda, recruit members, and organize members. The Internet and other communication technologies are also being used to send covert instructions on specific targets, tactics, bomb-making techniques, and other detailed information.

As new technologies emerge that make it easier to communicate and coordinate actions, terrorists are expected to take advantage of these high-tech advances to plan and carry out their activities. Technology may also create new weapons for terrorists to use.

With some scientific training and knowledge, terror groups might be able to convert some existing technologies into useable weapons. For example, electromagnetic pulse technologies (EMP) use an electromagnetic burst from a generator to disable electronic components such as microchips. On a large scale, EMP could be turned into a weapon used to destroy large amounts of military or financial information.

Improvements in plastics could mean the creation of weapons that could escape detection by metal detectors. Even chemicals that weaken metals might one day be made into weapons that could be applied to an enemy's vehicles and aircraft.

At the same time, new technologies can help law enforcement prevent and investigate terror attacks. While terrorists use the Internet and social media, law enforcement and intelligence agencies are also working the same sites, looking to identify and disrupt potential terror plots and suspects. Improvements in surveillance and security technologies could also strengthen defenses against terrorism.

In 2012, the FBI rolled out Sentinel, an information and case management software system, to all employees. With Sentinel, FBI agents maintain all documents for a case file digitally, which allows agents to easily link to related cases through digital search features. Sentinel's electronic workflow also makes important intelligence available to agents and analysts more quickly, which can allow agents to act on a threat before a suspect carries out an act of terror.

RECOVERY PLAN

The world's top psychiatrists have developed a five-point strategy for survivors dealing with traumatic events.

1. Take visible action to make terror attacks less likely by improving and increasing security.

2. Keep community members calm.

3. Enable connections—people need to connect with family and friends to reassure them that they are safe after an attack.

4. Foster a sense of community help—make resources available, such as phone numbers for counseling and other aid.

5. Encourage a sense of hope to repair the shattered view of the world that often comes after a major terror event.

Given the right support, communities that experience even the most horrific terror attacks can rise and recover.

PARTNERING WITH LOCAL COMMUNITIES

Working with local communities is considered to be a critical piece of successfully fighting and preventing terrorism. People in the community, schools, and local police are more likely to notice when a person begins to embrace extremist convictions and behaviors.

By intervening early, before a person commits a violent act, terrorism can be prevented for years into the future.

Fighting in Afghanistan has continued since 2001

credit: Spc. Christopher Baker, Department of Defense

In Rotterdam, the second-largest city in the Netherlands, religious leaders, community groups, and police are working to fight the threat of homegrown radicalism. Marianne Vorthoren runs SPIOR, an Islamic organization that works with imams, social workers, teachers, and community leaders to talk to youth and parents about radicalization. In 2016, SPIOR organized more than 40 meetings in Rotterdam to discuss radicalization. In the meetings, leaders try to boost resistance to radicalization.

> They expose the myths found in typical recruiting messages and talk about the factors that might motivate some people to become radicalized.

Rotterdam community police have developed strong personal relationships with residents. If an issue comes up, people feel comfortable calling the police for help.

When 30-year-old Mahmoud Tighadouini began to show signs of radicalization, his mother called the community police to intervene. An officer came to the house and confronted Tighadouini. He talked with Tighadouini and convinced him to cancel his plans to travel to Afghanistan to fight. Although he was initially very upset, Tighadouini says that the officer was very clear, and listening to the police helped him start to de-radicalize.

RECOVERING FROM TERRORISM

After recent terrorist attacks in France, England, and the United States, people around the world have felt fearful and threatened. They have wondered, "Why?"

A trusting relationship between the community and law enforcement is an essential part of combatting terrorism. What can both parties do to achieve this kind of respectful alliance?

Not only are victims and survivors of the attack affected, so also are their friends and family members. Exposed to violent images broadcast on news outlets, people around the world feel the effects of a terror attack. They become fearful, wondering where and when the next attack will strike.

For some people, the trauma and fear leads to increased anxiety, post-traumatic stress disorder, and other mental health issues. However, research has shown that the majority of people affected by terrorism are able to overcome their fears.

After a terror attack, people often come together as a community to form stronger bonds than before the attack occurred. These connections can be seen at the candlelight vigils and memorial services in which community members come together to support each other. After the terrorist bombings in Paris, the global community came together and demonstrated their support for France when millions of Facebook users changed their profile picture to include the French flag.

Although terror attacks can be devastating, they can also bring a community together, proving that the human race is incredibly resilient.

Michael Wright was a 30-year-old account executive working on the 81st floor of Tower One of the World Trade Center when the terrorist-flown airliner hit the building on 9/11. He struggled to make it out of the building alive and was traumatized by the death and destruction all around him.

MICHAEL'S STORY

You can read more about Michael Wright's experiences during and after 9/11 in this article. Do you think Wright's responses were typical of survivors? Do you think everyone responds to terror differently?

Michael Wright

In his words, the strength of the human spirit in the face of terror shines through.

"When we got back to my place, I collapsed and it all hit me. I cried like I've never cried in my life. I finally let loose, and it felt better. My brother helped me pack, and we got to Westchester, where my wife and family had gone. . . . My mother was there. My dad. My father-in-law. They all hugged me. Then they gave me my son. . . . I hugged him and sort of started the healing process there. Later, I went to Maine to sit by the ocean for a few days and get my head together. I saw all of my old friends. It was amazing. Everyone I know in my life has called me to tell me they love me. It's like having your funeral without having to die."[3]

Terrorism is certain to remain a threat to people and communities around the world for years to come. By understanding the history and motivations that drive terrorism, communities can work together to address the underlying factors that lead to terrorism. By working together with people from other backgrounds, faiths, and nationalities, we can all be part of the effort to promote peace and understanding.

KEY QUESTIONS

- Why did terrorist activity within the United States increase immediately after the 2016 presidential election?
- Why might lone wolf attacks have increased in frequency in recent times?
- What are some things you can do to help defeat terrorism, no matter where you live? How can you be a part of improving global relations?

CAN WE DO MORE?

Although law enforcement and intelligence agencies have been successful in stopping many terrorists before they act, there is often little coordination for the various counterterrorism initiatives at the local, state, and federal levels, which can allow a terror suspect to slip through the cracks.

In addition, little has been done to address the causes of terrorism. Rather than trying to prevent an attack after a person has become an extremist, a more effective prevention strategy could address the factors that lead an individual to become a violent extremist. Factors such as social alienation, psychological disorders, political grievances, and foreign terror group ideologies could be addressed and mitigated before a plan of violence even begins.

To investigate more, consider that sometimes memorials cause controversy. Research controversial memorials and learn about each side of the argument. Which do you agree with?

CREATE A MEMORIAL

Throughout the world, many memorials have been built to honor the victims of terrorist attacks. Some memorials display artifacts, while others feature sculpture or other art to express feelings. Some art expresses pain and grief, while other art focuses on new life and hope.

- **You can view some examples of memorials here.**

  9/11 Memorial

  Oklahoma City Outdoor Symbolic Memorial

  Great Monuments and Memorials of Terrorist Attacks Around the World

- **Using what you have learned about terrorism, design and create a memorial to the victims and survivors of terrorism.** You can choose to focus on a specific terror attack or create a general terrorism memorial. Consider the following in your design.

  - What form will you use?

  - Who is your intended audience?

  - What message or feeling are you trying to convey?

  - Will you use symbols in your memorial? What will they represent?

- **Share your memorial with classmates, friends, and family.** See if they can guess the meaning and message behind the memorial.

MONITORING THE SITUATION

Terrorism is a continuing threat in the modern world. One of the world's greatest terror threats comes from ISIS. In this activity, you will follow the actions of this group and analyze its motives, tactics, activities, and how the group is evolving.

- **During a one- to two-month period, follow ISIS in the news.** Find several sources of information about the group and its activities. Why is it important to access more than one source? How can you know if a resource is trustworthy and unbiased?

- **Each week, prepare a brief update about the terror group.** At the end of the period, consider the following questions.

  - How has the crisis with ISIS evolved during the past one to two months?

  - Have conditions gotten better or worse?

  - How has the United States, the UN, and the international community responded?

  - Have the positions of the international community changed at all?

  - What are the challenges faced by people living in areas controlled by ISIS?

  - Is there ongoing violence in the region?

  - Do you believe the conflict will end soon? Explain.

  - What do you think needs to happen in order to end the conflict? Is that solution realistic? Why or why not?

- **Prepare a presentation about what you have learned.**

> **To investigate more,** compare the threat of ISIS to another terror group. Why do you think analysts have called ISIS the greatest terror threat in the world? What characteristics make it more dangerous than other groups?

FINDING COMMON GROUND

Throughout history, people of different ethnic backgrounds, nationalities, races, and religions have regarded each other with distrust and fear. Many times, this fear comes from a lack of understanding about the other group and its beliefs and practices. For example, many non-Muslims in the Western world fear people who practice Islam, even though Islam is a peaceful religion. How can you promote understanding between people of different backgrounds?

- **Think about the ways misunderstandings arise between different backgrounds.** Choose two groups in conflict to research—consider religious, ethnic, racial, economic views. Examples include Christian/ Muslim, Muslim/Jew, Immigrant/Non-immigrant, Israeli/Palestinian. What differences exist that have created gaps in understanding between these two groups? What is the point of view of a person from each side?

- **Think about ways that you could promote understanding and reduce animosity between people of the two groups.** Come up with at least three proposals.

- **Write a brief essay that explains your plan to find common ground between the groups.** Be sure to include an introductory paragraph, separate paragraphs for each of your three main points, and a conclusion. Share your essay with your class.

To investigate more, choose another pair of groups and repeat the activity to find common ground.

activist: a person who fights for change.

adapt: to change one's behavior to fit into a new environment.

allies: people, groups, or states that have joined together for mutual benefit.

Al-Qaeda: an Islamic fundamentalist terror group that has carried out numerous acts of terror, including the 9/11 attacks in the United States.

ANFO explosives: explosives made from a mixture of ammonium nitrate and fuel oil.

anthrax: an infection caused by the bacterium *Bacillus anthracis*.

anti-Semitism: hostility toward people who practice Judaism.

apocalyptic: describing or predicting the complete destruction of the world.

aristocrat: a member of a ruling or wealthy class of people.

arson: the criminal act of deliberately setting fire to property.

artifact: an object made by people from past cultures, including tools, pottery, and jewelry.

autonomy: the right of self-government.

biological agent: a bacterium, virus, protozoan, parasite, or fungus that can be used purposefully as a weapon.

capitalism: an economy in which people, not the government, own the factories, ships, and land used in the production and distribution of goods.

caliphate: the rule or reign of a caliph or chief Muslim ruler.

casualty: a person who is injured or killed in battle.

CE: put after a date, CE stands for Common Era and counts up from zero. BCE stands for Before the Common Era and counts down to zero. These are non-religious terms that correspond to AD and BC.

ceasefire: a stoppage in fighting.

checkpoint: a barrier or manned entrance, typically at a border, where travelers are subject to security checks.

chemical agent: a chemical substance whose toxic properties are used to kill, injure, or incapacitate human beings.

Christianity: a religion whose followers, called Christians, believe that Jesus Christ is the son of God.

citizen: a person who legally belongs to a country and has the rights and protection of that country.

civilian: a person not in the armed forces or police.

cleric: a priest or religious leader, especially a Christian or Muslim one.

coded language: words that have a specific meaning to a certain group.

coerce: to persuade someone to do something by using force or threats.

commercial: relating to the buying and selling of goods or services, with the purpose of making money.

communism: an economy in which the government owns everything used in the production and distribution of goods.

corrupting: to cause to change from good to bad in morals, manners, or actions.

counterterrorism: political or military activities designed to prevent or thwart terrorism.

covert operation: an operation planned and executed to conceal the identity of or permit plausible denial by the sponsor.

culture: the beliefs and way of life of a group of people.

debate: a discussion between people with differing viewpoints.

debris: scattered pieces of waste or remains.

decentralize: to disperse or cause power to scatter from a central place.

dehumanize: to take away positive human qualities.

democracy: a government elected freely by the people.

derogatory: a critical or disrespectful attitude.

detonate: to explode or cause to explode.

detritus: loose bits of rock or cement.

dirty bomb: a bomb designed to release radioactive material when it is detonated.

discriminate: to unfairly treat a person or group differently from others, usually because of their race, gender, or age.

GLOSSARY

disinformation: intentionally false or misleading information intended to deceive a target audience.

doctrine: a set of beliefs held by a religious group.

domestic: existing or occurring inside a particular country.

due process: fair treatment through the normal judicial system, especially as a citizen's entitlement.

economic sanctions: commercial and financial penalties applied by one or more countries against a targeted country, group, or individual.

eco-terrorist: a terrorist motivated by a desire to protect the environment.

emigration: leaving one's own country in order to settle in another country.

emotion: a strong feeling about something or somebody.

enhanced interrogation: a group of interrogation techniques that some people believe are torture.

ethical: acting in a way that upholds someone's belief in right and wrong.

ethnic: relating to a group of people who share a common national, racial, or religious background.

ethno-nationalism: support for the interests of a particular ethnic group, especially with regard to its national independence or self-determination.

evacuate: to leave a dangerous place to go to a safe place.

evolve: to change or develop slowly, through time.

exile: to be away from one's home.

export: a good sent to another country for sale.

extort: to obtain something by force, threats, or other unfair means.

extradite: to hand over a person accused or convicted of a crime to the jurisdiction of the foreign state in which the crime was committed.

extremism: the holding of extreme political or religious views.

faction: a small, organized, dissenting group within a larger one, especially in politics.

fanatic: a person obsessed with an extreme religious or political cause.

fatwa: a ruling on a point of Islamic law given by a recognized authority.

freedom fighter: one who fights against oppression.

generalization: a general statement or concept obtained by inference from specific cases.

global: relating to the entire world.

granary: a building or room used to store grain.

guerrilla warfare: a form of irregular warfare in which a small group of combatants uses military tactics including ambushes, sabotage, raids, and hit-and-run tactics to fight a larger and less-mobile traditional military.

heritage: the cultural traditions and history of a group of people.

Hezbollah: a Shi'a Islamist militant group and political party based in Lebanon.

hijack: to unlawfully take control of an airplane, boat, or other vehicle.

Hindu: a follower of Hinduism, a group of religious beliefs, traditions, and practices from South Asia.

hostage: a person held against their will by another person or group in order to ensure demands are met.

humanitarian: having to do with helping the welfare or happiness of people.

human rights: basic rights that belong to every person.

ideology: a set of opinions or beliefs.

immoral: not conforming to accepted standards of morality.

imports: goods and services that are brought into a country for purchase.

improvised: created with little preparation using materials easily obtained.

indifferent: having no particular interest or concern.

industrialization: when there is a lot of manufacturing, with products made by machines in large factories.

inequality: differences in opportunity and treatment based on social, ethnic, racial, or economic qualities.

infidel: a person who does not believe in religion or who adheres to a religion other than one's own.

infiltrate: to enter or gain access to an organization or place sneakily and gradually, especially in order to acquire secret information.

inflammatory: speech or writing that arouses or is intended to arouse angry or violent feelings.

infrastructure: the basic physical and organizational structures and facilities, such as buildings, roads, and power supplies, needed for the operation of a society or enterprise.

injustice: unfair treatment of someone.

insurgent: a person who rises in forcible opposition to lawful authority.

intelligence: information and data gathered about a person, group, or other target.

intimidate: to make someone fearful.

intolerance: the unwillingness to accept views, beliefs, or behavior that differ from one's own.

invasion: entering a country or region with an armed force.

Islam: the religion founded by the prophet Mohammed, whose followers are called Muslims.

Islamic fundamentalism: a belief in the literal interpretation of Islam's sacred scripture, including a code of conduct.

jihad: a struggle or fight against the enemies of Islam.

Judaism: a religion developed by ancient Hebrews who believed in one god. Followers of Judaism are called Jews.

justify: to prove or show evidence that something is right.

left wing: the liberal, socialist, or radical section of a political party or system.

literal: the basic meaning of words.

lone wolf: a terrorist that acts alone.

manifesto: a published verbal declaration of the intentions, motives, or views of the issuer.

martyr: a person who endures great suffering and death for his or her religious beliefs.

militant: combative and aggressive in support of a political or social cause.

militia group: a subgroup of right-wing extremism that is typically organized in a paramilitary structure.

minority: a group of people that is smaller than or different from the larger group.

monarchy: a form of government where all power is given to a single individual, a king or queen.

moral absolutes: an ethical view that particular actions are intrinsically right or wrong.

motive: the reason or reasons one has for acting or behaving in a particular way.

mufti: a Muslim legal expert who is empowered to give rulings on religious matters.

Muslim: a person who practices Islam as a religion.

nationalism: an extreme form of patriotism, especially marked by a feeling of superiority over other countries.

nationality: the status of belonging to a particular nation.

negotiation: a discussion aimed at reaching an agreement.

neo-Nazi: a subgroup of right-wing extremism that follows principles from Nazi doctrine and are typically anti-Semitic.

nuclear weapon: a powerful weapon that uses the energy released by the splitting of atoms.

objective: a goal.

occupation: the seizure and control of an area.

offensive: causing someone to feel deeply hurt, upset, or angry.

oppression: an unjust or cruel exercise of authority and power.

organism: any living thing, such as a plant or animal.

pan-Islamic: a political movement advocating the unity of Muslims under one Islamic state.

paramilitary: a group that is organized like a military force, but is not part of the official armed forces.

petition: a request to do something, most commonly addressed to a government official or public entity.

phenomenon: an observable fact or event.

pipe bomb: a bomb made from explosives packed inside a hollow pipe.

GLOSSARY

plastic explosive: a soft and hand-moldable solid form of explosive material.

political: relating to running a government and holding onto power.

post-traumatic stress syndrome: a psychological reaction to a stressful event that can involve depression, anxiety, flashbacks, and nightmares.

profiling: the act of suspecting or targeting a person on the basis of observed characteristics or behavior.

propaganda: information, especially of a biased or misleading nature, used to promote a political cause or point of view.

prophet: a person who claims to speak for God.

psychological damage: a type of damage to the mind that occurs as a result of a severely distressing event.

punitive strike: a military action taken to punish a state or any group of persons.

race war: conflict between two or more races.

racial: relating to race.

racism: negative opinions or treatment of people based on race.

racist: describes the hatred of people of a different race.

radical: a person with extreme political or social views.

radicalization: the action or process of causing someone to adopt radical positions on political or social issues.

radiological agent: a radioactive material or radiation released that has adverse health effects.

ransom: a payment demanded in exchange for releasing a captive.

recruit: to enlist new people to a cause or army.

refugee: someone escaping war, persecution, or natural disaster.

renounce: to give up.

repressive: inhibiting or restraining the freedom of a person or group of people.

resistance: a force that slows down another force.

resolution: a formal expression of opinion, will, or intent voted by an official body or assembled group.

retaliation: the act of seeking revenge.

revolutionary: a person committed to fighting a ruler or political system.

right wing: the conservative or reactionary section of a political party or system.

righteous: morally right or justified.

rubble: broken fragments of stone and other matter caused by the destruction of a building.

sabotage: to deliberately destroy, damage, or obstruct something, especially for political or military advantage.

sacred texts: the primary texts relating to a religion.

secular: not religious.

self-determination: the right of a people to independence and to choose their form of government.

sexism: negative opinions or treatment of people based on gender.

Shi'a: the smaller of the two main groups of Muslims.

skinhead: a young man of a subculture characterized by close-cropped hair and heavy boots, often perceived as aggressive.

social: living in groups.

social alienation: the state or experience of being isolated from a group or an activity to which one should belong or in which one should be involved.

socialist: describes a system that combines capitalist and communist methods. The government provides services, but private property is allowed.

socio-economic: the interaction of social and economic factors.

sovereign citizen: a subgroup of right-wing extremism that believes the government has no authority over them.

state sanctioned: encouraged or permitted by a country or government.

status quo: the existing state of affairs.

stereotype: a judgment about a group of individuals or the inaccurate belief that all people who share a single physical or cultural trait are the same.

stockpile: to accumulate a large amount of goods and materials.

suicide bomber: an attacker who expects to die during his or her attack.

suicide mission: a task so dangerous for the people involved that they are not expected to survive.

Sunni: the larger of the two main groups of Muslims.

superiority: a higher quality, accomplishment, or significance.

supremacy: the position of being accepted or established as superior to all others in some field or activity.

surveillance: close observation of a person or place.

symbolic target: a target that has special meaning to a community.

tactic: a carefully planned action or strategy to achieve something.

terrorism: the unlawful use of violence and intimidation, especially against civilians, in the pursuit of political aims.

terrorist: someone who causes panic and anxiety as a way of controlling people.

the West: refers to countries whose history is strongly marked by European immigration or settlement, such as the Americas, as well as Europe.

theological: having to do with the study of religion or ideas about religion.

trade restrictions: limits on the amount of trade between two countries.

undercover: working secretly within a community or organization, often to spy or gather information.

USA Patriot Act: an act of Congress that was signed into law in 2001 that expands law enforcement's ability to detect and prevent possible acts of terrorism or sponsorship of terrorist groups.

vandalism: action involving deliberate destruction of or damage to public or private property.

violence: physical force intended to hurt, damage, or kill someone or something.

weapon of mass destruction: a chemical, biological, nuclear, or radioactive weapon capable of causing widespread death and destruction.

white supremacy: the belief that white people are superior to those of all other races.

xenophobia: an intense or irrational dislike or fear of people from other countries.

RESOURCES

BOOKS

Bergen, Peter *United States of Jihad: Investigating America's Homegrown Terrorists*. Crown, 2016.

Byman, Daniel. *Al-Qaeda, the Islamic State, and the Global Jihadist Movement*. Oxford University Press, 2015.

Combs, Cynthia C. *Terrorism in the Twenty-First Century*. 7th ed. Pearson, 2012.

Gabriel, Mark A. *Islam and Terrorism*. Frontline, 2015.

Law, Randall D., ed. *The Routledge History of Terrorism*. Routledge, 2015.

Levin, John, and Jack Levin. *Domestic Terrorism*. Chelsea House, 2006.

Henningfeld, Diane Andrews. *The Oklahoma City Bombing*. Greenhaven, 2012.

Morell, Michael. *The Great War of Our Time: The CIA's Fight Against Terrorism from al Qa'ida to ISIS*. Hachette Book Group, 2015.

Simon, Jeffrey D. *Lone Wolf Terrorism: Understanding the Growing Threat*. Prometheus Books, 2013.

MUSEUMS AND MEMORIALS

National September 11 Memorial & Museum 911memorial.org/museum

Lockerbie Garden of Remembrance undiscoveredscotland.co.uk/lockerbie/gardenofremembrance

The National Museum of Crime and Punishment crimemuseum.org/crime-library/terrorism

Oklahoma City National Memorial & Museum oklahomacitynationalmemorial.org

WEBSITES

Amnesty International amnestyusa.org

Anti-Defamation League – Combating Hate adl.org/combating-hate

Federal Bureau of Investigation fbi.gov

Human Rights Watch hrw.org

RAND Corporation rand.org

Southern Poverty Law Center – Hate and Extremism splcenter.org/what-we-do/hate-and-extremism

United Nations Security Council Counter-Terrorism Committee un.org/sc/ctc

U.S. Department of Homeland Security dhs.gov

QR CODE GLOSSARY

Page 5: telegraph.co.uk/news/worldnews/september-11-attacks/10832749/911-Museum-in-pictures-National-September-11-Memorial-opens-in-New-York.html?frame=2911890

Page 17: start.umd.edu/gtd/images/START_GlobalTerrorismDatabase_TerroristAttacksConcentrationIntensityMap_45Years.png

Page 42: bbc.com/news/world-middle-east-14628835

Page 42: news.trust.org//spotlight/Israeli-Palestinian-conflict/?tab=briefing

Page 42: jewishpost.com/archives/news/Life-on-a-West-Bank-Settlement.html

Page 42: ifamericaknew.org/cur_sit/ref-halsell.html

Page 53: nytimes.com/2017/04/07/opinion/what-its-like-to-survive-a-sarin-gas-attack.html?_r=0

Page 76: nytimes.com/2015/06/28/world/americas/isis-online-recruiting-american.html

Page 76: cnn.com/2015/03/27/us/tsarnaev-13th-juror-jahar-radicalization

Page 76: rollingstone.com/culture/features/teenage-jihad-inside-the-world-of-american-kids-seduced-by-isis-20150325

Page 86: un.org/press/en/2001/sc7158.doc.htm

Page 89: dhs.gov/national-terrorism-advisory-system

Page 94: newsweek.com/debate-privacy-vs-security-resurfaces-following-paris-attacks-395722

Page 94: cnbc.com/2016/03/29/apple-vs-fbi-all-you-need-to-know.html

Page 94: pewresearch.org/fact-tank/2016/02/19/americans-feel-the-tensions-between-privacy-and-security-concerns

Page 95: heritage.org/terrorism/report/60-terrorist-plots-911-continued-lessons-domestic-counterterrorism

Page 99: wsj.com/video/iraq-isis-sparks-a-middle-east-crisis-explained/74607CBE-0725-4C02-A289-ABA34FEAB516.html#!74607CBE-0725-4C02-A289-ABA34FEAB516

Page 106: esquire.com/news-politics/a2038/esq0102-jan-wtc-rev

Page 108: oklahomacitynationalmemorial.org/about/outdoor-symbolic-memorial

Page 108: 911memorial.org/memorial

Page 108: designrulz.com/design/2015/02/great-monuments-memorials-terrorist-attacks-around-world

RESOURCES

SOURCE NOTES

CHAPTER 1

1 upi.com/Archives/1995/01/27/Hezbollah-mentor-urges-US-boycott/1443791182800

2 sourcebooks.fordham.edu/mod/robespierre-terror.asp

CHAPTER 2

1 Inside Terrorism

2 forbes.com/sites/dominicdudley/2016/11/18/countries-most-affected-by-terrorism/#184a262330d9

3 *Inside Terrorism*, pg 93 of 433, Loc 2161 of 10588

4 *Inside Terrorism*, pg 94 of 433, Loc 2190 of 10588

5 www2.heritage.org/research/projects/enemy-detention/al-qaeda-declarations

CHAPTER 3

1 bbc.com/news/world-europe-34813570

2 themighty.com/2016/09/experiencing-anxiety-after-911-as-a-new-yorker

3 bbc.com/news/uk-33253598

4 nytimes.com/2017/04/07/opinion/what-its-like-to-survive-a-sarin-gas-attack.html?_r=0

5 washingtontimes.com/news/2017/apr/9/suicide-bombers-kill-44-at-palm-sunday-services-in

CHAPTER 4

1 womenshealthmag.com/life/abortion-provider-interview

CHAPTER 5

1 fbi.gov/news/stories/stopping-a-suicide-bomber

2 cfr.org/terrorism/global-regime-terrorism/p25729#p1

CHAPTER 6

1 economicsandpeace.org/wp-content/uploads/2016/11/Global-Terrorism-Index-2016.2.pdf

2 start.umd.edu/publication/victims-ideological-homicides-1990-2014

3 esquire.com/news-politics/a2038/esq0102-jan-wtc-rev

INDEX

response to terrorism
    community partnerships
        and, 104–105
    economic sanctions
        as, 85–86, 88
    enhanced security
        procedures as, 84, 96
    future, 98–107
    intelligence analysis
        as, 81, 83, 90
    military force as, vii, 5, 6, 80–81
    negotiation as, 78–80
    privacy and civil rights
        concerns with, 92–94, 96
    recovery from terrorism
        and, 103, 105–107
    stopping attacks as,
        82–83, 88, 95, 101
    United Nations role in,
        vii, 85–88, 99
    United States' policies on,
        vi–vii, 5, 6, 7, 80–83,
        85, 88–96, 101, 103
right-wing groups, 39–40,
    62–64, 100, 101

S

September 11, 2001 terrorist
    attacks, vii, 2–8, 14, 18, 36,
    46, 49, 80–81, 86–87, 88,
    91–93, 106–107, 108
sovereign citizens, 63–64
suicide bombers, vi–vii, 17,
    18, 32, 36, 44, 46–47, 49,
    51, 54–55, 82–83, 101
Syria, vii, 16, 17, 53, 73, 99–100

T

tactics and targets
    audience for, 48
    cyberterrorism as, 56
    example of, 44–45
    funding strategies as, 55
    methods of attack, 49

objective of, 45–47
    suicide bombers as, 44,
        46–47, 49, 51, 54–55. See
        also suicide bombers
    target selection, 48, 49
    terrorism defined by
        choice of, 10–11
    weapons for, 50–54. See
        also bombs/bombings
Taliban, 30, 31, 88
terrorism
    defining, 10–22
    forms of, 14–15
    future of. See future of terrorism
    history of, vi–vii, 3, 7, 17–18
    response to. See response
        to terrorism
    tactics and targets of. See
        tactics and targets
    terrorists performing.
        See terrorists
    United States and. See
        United States
terrorists
    cyber- or high tech terrorists
        as, 56, 102–103
    decentralized operations of, 101
    eco-terrorists as, 71–72
    ethno-nationalist motivations of,
        25–27, 37–38, 45. See also
        racial and ethnic extremism
    financing of, 55, 100
    freedom fighters vs., 15–16, 22
    lone wolf, 67–69, 102
    mixed motivations of, 37–38
    political motivations of, 38–40.
        See also political extremism
    radicalization of, 72–76, 105
    religious motivations of,
        25, 27–38, 39. See also
        religious extremism
    varied backgrounds of, 24, 41

U

United Kingdom, vi, vii,
    37–38, 46–47, 79

United Nations, vii, 85–88, 99
United States
    eco-terrorists in, 71–72
    extremism in, 12,
        61–67, 100–101
    FBI of, 10, 52, 56, 62, 66,
        68, 81, 82–83, 89, 103
    Homeland Security of, vii, 88–89
    intelligence agencies of, 90
    Islamic fundamentalists
        opposing, vi, 32–33, 35–36
    lone wolf terrorists in, 67–69
    military force of, vii, 5, 6,
        7, 15, 16, 80–81
    politically motivated terrorists
        in, 62–64, 69–70, 100, 101
    privacy and civil rights
        issues in, 92–94, 96
    racially motived terrorists
        in, 60, 65–67, 68
    radicalization in, 72–75
    religiously motivated terrorists
        in, 61–62, 64–65, 100–101
    response to terrorism by,
        vi–vii, 5, 6, 7, 80–83,
        85, 88–96, 101, 103
    terrorism in, vi–vii, 2–8,
        16, 17, 18, 29, 32, 36,
        46, 50, 51, 52, 60–76,
        100–101, 106–107, 108
    terrorist attacks on international
        targets from, vi, 6, 7,
        30, 32, 33, 36, 55
    USA Patriot Act in, vii, 91–92
USS Cole attacks, 7, 36

W

weapons, 50–54. See also
    bombs/bombings
white supremacists, 12,
    14, 65–67, 68

Z

Zealots, vi, 28